CROSSROADS

Also by Harry Samuels

BESHERT: TRUE STORIES OF CONNECTIONS

CROSSROADS

Chance or Destiny?

true short stories

Harry Samuels

Foreword by
Rabbi Harry K. Danziger

iUniverse, Inc.
New York Lincoln Shanghai

CROSSROADS
Chance or Destiny?

Copyright © 2007 by Harry Samuels

iUniverse books may be ordered through booksellers or by contacting:

iUniverse
2021 Pine Lake Road, Suite 100
Lincoln, NE 68512
www.iuniverse.com
1-800-Authors (1-800-288-4677)

ISBN: 978-0-595-42579-2 (pbk)
ISBN: 978-0-595-86908-4 (ebk)

Printed in the United States of America

For our three wonderful grandchildren;
Mirel, Dovid and Yehudis:
Delight in the present and hope for the future.

It is not good that man should be alone.

—Genesis 11:18

All things are connected like the blood that unites us.
We did not weave the web of life. We are only strands in it.

—Chief Seattle

CONTENTS

Part II   *LOVE STORIES*

Part VIII ISRAEL

ACKNOWLEDGMENTS

Not only is Natalie Jalenak a good friend and bridge player, but her proof reading and editorial suggestions have been invaluable.

May Lynn Mansbach graciously provided editorial suggestions for which I am most appreciative.

Irma Sheon and Flora Samuels were early reviewers of my manuscript as well as contributors of stories.

Whether serving as rabbi emeritus of Temple Israel in Memphis or president of the Central Conference of American Rabbis, representing the largest rabbinical organization in America, Rabbi Harry K. Danziger is a class act. When I asked him to write the *Forward* for *Crossroads*, his response was, "You have honored me by asking." We are all honored to have him as our rabbi, friend and national leader.

Gilbert Halpern and Rabbi Levi Klein have again helped a computer challenged friend.

My thanks and gratitude to the following contributors of stories and recommendations:

Aaron Balkin, Sue Balkin, Warren Brashear, Jeff Baum, Dee Bloom, Joel Braverman, Deanna Burson, Gene Camerik, Brad Cohen, Rishe Deitsch, Hannah Deutscher, Bill Eaton, Dr. Yehudah Farkash, Joel Felt, Marilyn Fox, Sam Fox, Pam Frenzel, Theo Garb, Aviva Garfine, Dr. Edward Glick, Baruch Gordon, Jon Greenberg, Thelma Waller Greenberg, Rabbi Efraim Greenblatt, Rabbi Rafael Grossman, Murray Habbaz, James B. Jalenak, Rabbi Rafael Kahn, Rabbi Yosef Kantor, Tamar Kasher, Eugene Katz, Rivky Klein, Louis Kotler, Dr. Sidney Kriger, Leonard Newman, Jane Lettes, Dr. Joe Levy, Edward Lindberg, Marilyn Lipman, Miller Loosier, Alvin Malnik, Rabbi Chaim Mentz, Heidi Newman, Dr. David Patterson, Rabbi Shlomo Riskin, Ted Roberts, Herman Rosenblatt, Dr. Jacob Rosensweig, Bob Rosenthal, Zev Roth, Friderica Saharovici, Leonid Saharovici, Flora Samuels, William Samuels, Dr. Norman Shapiro, Irma Sheon, Lara Shwer, Shelley Smuckler, Gina Sugarmon, Sharon Tabachnick, Chana Weisberg, Marilyn Zellner, Rabbi Binyamin Zilberstrom.

All proceeds received by the author will be donated to charity.

Harry Samuels

FOREWORD

Rabbi Harry K. Danziger

A hurricane strikes Miami Beach in August 1964. A college student cannot use the hotel's typewriter and mimeograph machine for a student government project for the fall. The hotel loses power; guests sleep in the hallways; vacations are ruined. But, as the saying goes, "It's an ill wind that blows no good."

That college student returns to Memphis and goes to her temple to use the mimeograph machine. The new young assistant rabbi hears someone in an unoccupied office and goes to see what is happening. Out of that hurricane in South Florida grows my wife's and my marriage of over forty years.

People throughout America and beyond have come to know of Harry Samuels. They bring him their personal stories of the unlikely and "beyond probability." He shares them with us as he gives to so many people in many and varied ways.

In most stories, there are happy endings to what might have been unhappy situations. In others, there are unexpected encounters between people who are connected to one another yet would likely never have met. In some vignettes, there is sadness. But the overwhelming impact of these stories is a sense of hope. Good things—unlikely and improbable—may come even out of our darkest times.

One question remains unanswered. Are these chance occasions, coincidences, only happenstance? When we say, "It's a small world" after meeting a cousin's roommate's parents because we and they were stranded by airline delays, is it only the operation of what some call "six degrees of separation"? Are these seemingly unusual experiences to be expected in the countless events and encounters of which life is made up? Harry Samuels does not dodge that question. In his *Afterword*, he cites authors and scholars who explain what he calls synchronicities as simply the operation of randomness or chance.

But that is not his position. He clearly believes that these "happy coincidences" are the result of conscious power acting in human experience. As he puts it so poetically, "To me life is a divine symphony—all under the direction of the Composer who is the only one who knows the entire score."

Some of us cannot subscribe to the belief that the Composer chooses one person to be delayed in getting to work on 9/11/2001 while another arrives at his office because an appointment was cancelled. Some of us cannot believe that there is a higher and unknown purpose behind one person's missing a plane and living while hundreds of others make the plane and perish.

But those who do believe in that "Composer" and that "score" remind us of what may be the ultimate human enterprise: finding meaning and pattern in the kaleidoscope of life's experiences. More than one philosopher or thinker has said that our greatest challenge is to overcome the fear that life is meaningless and that we are actors in a theater of the absurd. Harry Samuels passionately believes that there is meaning, hope and goodness at the heart of life, and he enriches his readers with the stories he collects and the faith he professes. He causes us to look into our own lives for experiences that, yes, could be called coincidence but, then again, could be celebrated as a divine power working invisibly.

I am one who cannot embrace the idea that God or the Composer picks and chooses so that one person survives and another dies. At the same time, there is a part of me that demands that the sum total of life be more than a collection of mere chance happenings.

Harry Samuels says that his books "are not meant to answer questions but rather to raise them." I thank him for raising them again for me.

On reaching the end of *Crossroads*, I suddenly was reminded of one of my favorite moments in the movies.

In a film called *Lies My Father Told Me*, a young child rides with his grandfather on the wagon from which the grandfather sells his wares. "Zayde (Grandfather)," asks the child, "Do you believe in miracles?"

"Do I believe in miracles? No. I don't believe in them, but I rely on them."

On reading Harry Samuels's stories, a voice in me says, "Don't we all?"

Rabbi Harry K Danziger
Memphis Tennessee

INTRODUCTION

Harry Samuels

While visiting the Chautauqua Institution at Chautauqua, NY, during July 2004, I was invited to discuss my first book, *Beshert: True Stories of Connections*, in a radio interview. One other guest was being interviewed: Robert D. Putnam, Ph.D., and professor of sociology at Harvard.

Dr. Putnam, author of the best-selling book *Bowling Alone*, had come to Chautauqua to present his most recent book, *Better Together*. The thrust of his books is that since the mid-1940s our society has suffered greatly because we have become disconnected from each other. My book *Beshert*, like its sequel *Crossroads*, promotes outreach and offers true anecdotes that illustrate the synchronistic effects of people connecting with each other. In *Vienna Revisited*, for example, a strong compulsion to cross a bridge leads to a mind-boggling event.

Coincidence describes accidental and remarkable events or ideas that appear to be connected but lack a causal relationship while synchronicity, according to Carl Jung, is "the *meaningful* coincidence of two or more events where probability or chance is not involved." Synchronicity, thus defined, implies purpose rather than randomness, and it is this concept that best describes many of the incidents included in this book.

Some of the stories involve interesting and unlikely events that might also be attributed to probability. Whether synchronicity is at play is not known, but even the less dramatic of these stories demonstrate the fact that our world is indeed quite small.

Following our interviews, Dr. Putnam and I chatted. I was conscious of the obvious disparity between us. Dr. Putnam's credentials and expertise are well known and, as a sought-after authority, he was scheduled that day to address six thousand people in the Chautauqua amphitheater. I, unknown and untested, had brought my yet unpublished manuscript to Chautauqua at the request of fourteen friends. Nevertheless, those who heard our radio interview suggested that *Beshert* seemed to be a microcosmic response to Dr. Putnam's indictment of modern society. This observation, which surprised and delighted me at the time, continues to be confirmed by feedback from readers who believe it to be similarly applicable to *Crossroads*. Following are some of their comments:

1, "Your book promotes a community spirit of reaching out to others and thereby making friends."

2, "As one who has suffered recent loss, you have encouraged me to reach out to others who are also suffering, thereby helping us both."

3, "As a hospice patient, I find your stories comforting inasmuch as they suggest purpose in our life experiences."

4, "Let me tell you about *Beshert*," one reader said. "The day I decided to read it I was very depressed, but when I began, it lifted my spirits."

5. Several high school teachers and a Methodist youth minister have said they were using the text in their classes.

The creation of *Beshert* and *Crossroads* has produced countless heartwarming experiences for my wife and me. We have marveled that meanings we overlooked continue to be discovered by readers. The new friends with whom we have connected while mining for material to include in the books have been a source of amazement and joy, pleasures I hope you will share as you read of their experiences.

These stories are divided into eight general categories. They are independent and relate to each other only as examples of the remarkable impact the participants in each story had on each other.

All of us have the ability to experience the synchronicity that is often the result of reaching out to others. Those of us who do not reach out often fail to do so because of shyness. Scott Ginsburg, author of *Hello, My Name is Scott*, discovered a great connecting mechanism simply by continuing to wear a nametag he had worn at a college seminar. Similarly, I have found that the use of the questions "Don't I know you?", "Where are you from?", or "Have we met before?" can lead to fascinating exchanges. I encourage you to try these words. The resulting connections can be magical. As Ben Harper puts it:

> *Speak kind to a stranger, because you never know—*
> *It just might be an angel, come knockin' at your door.*

Please join our journey into the world of synchronicity as we explore the question: Do the crossroads of our lives converge by chance or by destiny?

May you find these stories fascinating and thought-provoking. May they increase the awareness of your own synchronistic experiences, and may you be blessed with meaningful connections.

Harry Samuels
Memphis
2007

PART I
FAMILY

MOTHER KNOWS BEST

Eugene Katz

During the late 1920s when Prohibition was the law of the land, Abe Katz worked for the Chicago post office. He was seventeen and the few dollars he was paid to drive a truck helped pay the rent on his parents' apartment.

Joe, a friend and co-worker one day asked, "Would you like to earn some real money?"

"You know the answer to that question. What do I have to do?"

"Just what you're already doing—driving a truck at night," Joe replied. "The only difference is that this one belongs to Al Capone!"

"Are you nuts? I don't want to work for gangsters," Abe retorted. "That could be very dangerous to say the least, and besides I don't want to end up in prison."

"You don't understand, Abe," Joe continued, "when we travel to pick up some beer or whiskey, a police car leads us and another police car brings up the rear. It couldn't be safer."

Abe knew that some states such as New York refused to enforce prohibition and that the police protected Capone's trucks. It was a lot of money for the eager young man, and he agreed. He began driving for the post office during the day and for Mr. Capone at night. The combined paychecks were substantial.

One day his mother found his large stash of money—six hundred twenty-five dollars—while doing laundry in their apartment. Abe had hidden it with his underwear in his dresser. "What's this money doing here?" she demanded.

"I've been driving a truck for Mr. Capone," he reluctantly admitted, "but it's perfectly safe," he hurriedly assured her.

"You're going to stop immediately!" she demanded.

"But Mom," he pleaded, "just let me work one more week. We have a special haul tomorrow and our pay is going to double."

"Absolutely not," she insisted. "Call your boss right now and tell him you're through."

Grudgingly, he obeyed her. The following day he and two others were to have driven a truck to Detroit to pick up some smuggled Canadian whiskey for

George "Bugs" Moran. The other drivers met at a warehouse located at 2122 Clark Street. Some men dressed as policemen made them line up against a wall where they shot them. It was February 14, 1929—the date that made headlines throughout the country as *The St. Valentine's Day Massacre*.

THE PROFESSOR

Hannah Deutscher

After sharing stories with a group at the Chautauqua Institution in July 2006, I invited members of the audience to tell some of their own anecdotes that I might use in my next book. Mrs. Hannah Deutscher stunned us with this one. "I lived in Israel," she said, "at the time this incident was made public."

In 1939 Dovid, his wife, Natasha, and their one-year-old daughter Sofya lived in a small village near Levov, Poland. When the Nazis came, Dovid was caught and shipped to Auschwitz. Natasha and her daughter hid with neighbors on a nearby farm. After the war they moved to Israel and joined a kibbutz near Jerusalem. Natasha obtained a job with a bank while she searched desperately for her husband—finally accepting the fact that he had perished in the Holocaust.

As was the custom with most newcomers, they changed their names to divorce themselves from their brutal past and to become more readily absorbed into their new society. They became Tamar and Naomi, as they began to carve out a new life for themselves.

Years later Naomi began studying at a University in Jerusalem. One day she remarked to her mother, "I've met the most wonderful professor. His name is Barak Greenblatt, and he is everyone's favorite. I'm fortunate to be in his class."

The following week she told her mother, "He's absolutely charming, witty and handsome. I wish you could meet him."

A few weeks later she again mentioned Dr. Greenblatt. "He took me to dinner last night, and afterwards we talked for hours. I realize the disparity in our ages, but he is brilliant and extremely nice."

Tamar replied, "I want to meet this man before anything serious develops. Why don't you invite him here for dinner Thursday night?"

Barak drove to their home on the appointed day. With a bouquet of fresh flowers in hand he rang the doorbell. Naomi opened the door and greeted him, but before she could introduce him, her mother screamed and rushed into his arms. Between sobs and kisses she told her bewildered daughter, "This is your father!"

Barak had also changed his name. He had searched all of the records available for information of his wife and daughter and had concluded that they had perished. All of the names other than Hannah Deutscher are fictitious.

A JAR OF QUARTERS

Marilyn Lipman

On October 26, 2004 my wife and I met Marilyn Lipman who had traveled from New York. She shared the following incident with us:

"I realized that I had to do some laundry before coming to Memphis. I took my jar of quarters to the laundry room, loaded the washing machine, and stopped at a nearby coffee shop until the clothes were finished. As I sat drinking some coffee, a lady approached."

"Would you please sell me some quarters so I can launder my things?" she implored.

"I handed her the jar saying, help yourself. When she returned to reimburse me and to thank me for helping, I invited her to sit with me."

"You speak with an accent," I said. "Where are you from?"

"I am from Berlin," she replied. "Then from Auschwitz," she responded rolling up her sleeve and displaying the numbers tattooed on her arm.

"How did you survive? I questioned.

"There was a Nazi lieutenant by the name of Fritz[1] who took pity on me. He saved my life. My brother was in another camp, and an officer named Helmut[2], who shared the same last name as my benefactor, saved him. Both of us survived and came to America. I became a social worker and have been working for an adoption agency helping couples obtain Russian babies. Not long ago, a couple that had previously filed an application with our agency came to my office. As they entered, I announced their names."

"You are the first person to pronounce my obviously Teutonic name correctly," the man said.

"I couldn't forget that name," I replied. "Someone with that last name whose first name was Fritz saved my life in Auschwitz."

"He was my father!" the applicant announced.

"My brother was saved by someone named Helmut with the same last name," I added.

"He was my uncle, replied the young man.

---

1. Pseudonym
2. Pseudonym

THE TEACHER

Brad Cohen

Until we see someone who is afflicted, most of us accept our ability to function normally as a given, an entitlement. As Brad Cohen began to mature, he couldn't understand why he felt compelled to exhibit what his teachers termed, unacceptable behavior. He made strange noises and body movements. Only his mother, Ellen, his grandmother, Dorothy, and his brother, Jeff, supported him. To most of his peers, he was a social outcast. We now recognize his symptoms as the manifestation of a rare neurological disorder called Tourette Syndrome, but prior to a proper diagnosis his life was a living hell.

According to Brad, "My fifth grade teacher—who did not understand my problem—was so incensed with my behavior she humiliated me. One day she insisted I stand before my classmates and apologize for making noises. She then made me promise to stop. I knew I was making noises; how could I not know? But I didn't know why."

Of course, he couldn't stop—just as we cannot refrain from blinking. It was degrading to be forced to do this, but as he explains, "That teacher—unwittingly—had a huge positive impact on me. It was truly a synchronistic experience in my life. I vowed at that moment to become the teacher I never had. I would be a kind, caring, role model for young people and help make positive changes in their lives." And that is what happened.

Brad, who is my great-nephew, moved to Atlanta following his college graduation. He sought employment as a primary grade-school teacher in the public school system. Following his rejection by twenty-four school principals, he was, at last, given a position to teach a second grade class—notwithstanding concerns about the responses of the parents. A year later, while visiting my sister, his grandmother, in St. Louis, the telephone rang. It was Brad's mom. She mentioned that she had just returned from Washington D.C. "How is my friend, Brad? I inquired. "He's the reason I was in Washington," she replied. "Brad was selected as the most outstanding first year teacher in the state of Georgia, and I accompanied him to the capitol where he was honored for his achievements."

At the end of that school year, the parents of his students petitioned the principal to promote Brad to the third grade so their kids would have him as their teacher another year. The enthusiasm of his students was apparent when they spoke of Brad on Oprah's recent television show—where he received a standing ovation.

If you are interested in learning more about this remarkable individual and about Tourette Syndrome, read his autobiography: Front of the Class: How Tourette Syndrome Made Me the Teacher I Never Had. 2005. VanderWyk & Burnham. Acton, Mass. *It is inspirational to all who have been afflicted with Tourette Syndrome, and it is an enlightening message to their teachers. It is further inspiring to all who have felt handicapped by having received a "bad deal" from life.*

THE PLAY

Jane Lettes

Jane Lettes, who helped edit *Beshert,* had just returned from visiting her daughter, Jan, and her family in Atlanta. While there, she accompanied her granddaughter to a play. During the intermission, she spoke with May Lynn and Charles Mansbach from Memphis who also were accompanying their Atlanta granddaughter to the play, and with Hank Kimmelman and his daughter who lived in Atlanta.

It had only been a few months since the publication of my book, which introduced the concept of synchronicity in our life experiences. As they spoke to each other during the intermission, Hank said, "We have something in common. Each of us has a story in Harry's book!"

Upon her return to Memphis, Jane called to tell me of her experience. "This is not the end of the story," she exclaimed. "As I unpacked my suitcase, I noticed the playbill I had brought home. The name of the theater in Atlanta was 'Synchronicity!'"

CONNECTING IN MAINE

Harry Samuels

While driving along the magnificent Maine coast last year on a bright and sunny spring afternoon, we stopped for lunch at the charming community of Boothbay. I asked a friendly man standing on the pier, where we were taking pictures, if he lived in the city and, if so, the name of a good restaurant. He led us to a restaurant filled with good food and interesting people.

As we ascended the stairs following lunch, we saw two pug puppies on leashes held by a friendly lady. I began playing with her dogs. As we spoke, I detected a St. Louis, Missouri accent. "You don't sound like you're from around here," I said. "Where are you from?"

"I'm from St. Louis," she told us.

"What was your maiden name?" I inquired.

"Jacobs," she answered.

"I met Rabbi Robert Jacobs when I attended Washington University in St. Louis. He was the director of Hillel."(Jewish college youth organization.)

"He was no relation," she replied.

"There was a man by the name of Jacobs whom I never met, but of whom I heard many nice things," I offered. "He was the scoutmaster of my nephew's troop in University City, Missouri. He was such a role model that my nephew now serves as the scoutmaster of the largest scout troop in Kentucky."

"Dad was a scoutmaster, she said. "What's your nephew's name?"

"Dr. Stanley Frager," I replied.

"He was a pallbearer at my father's funeral!" she exclaimed, kissing my cheek.

Dr. Stanley R. Frager is a professor of psychology at the University of Louisville. He's the author of the book The Champion Within You: How to Overcome Problems, Obstacles, and Adversity in Your Life. *He is a highly regarded motivational speaker who has conducted seminars for some of the most outstanding corporations in the country.*

A MATCH

Rishe Deitsch

Mr. & Mrs. Cohen and their daughter, Batya, immigrated to Israel from South Africa. A short time later, Batya began suffering headaches. She was diagnosed with an inoperable brain tumor that resulted in her death at age eighteen.

A short time later, Mrs. Cohen was diagnosed with leukemia. Her condition appeared to be hopeless when a friend contacted Esther, a woman who worked with energy healing, a system of activating natural healing abilities of the body. When Esther visited Mrs. Cohen in the hospital, she found the patient very weak and sad. She had been told that her only hope was a bone-marrow transplant, but no match had been found. Her best chance was from a close blood relative, but none was alive.

After leaving the patient, Esther was asked to come next door to a maternity hospital to help a friend with her delivery. As she approached the nurse's station to learn the room number of her friend, she noticed a young pregnant woman in a wheelchair who was registering. She heard her say her name was Sara, and she seemed to have a strong resemblance to Mrs. Cohen, the sick woman she had just seen. The thought occurred to her that this young woman might be a suitable bone-marrow match, and she made a mental note to explore that possibility after her friend's delivery.

After leaving her friend's room, Esther approached one of the nurses to seek some information about the young woman she had seen registering earlier. She was told that this was Sara's first birth and that the couple had recently moved from South Africa. Esther asked, "Would you ask if she would be willing to be tested as a bone-marrow donor for someone?"

The nurse returned smiling," She would be happy to do so."

A few hours after Sara's delivery of a healthy baby girl, Esther introduced herself to the new mother and her husband. She explained the bone-marrow process and was relieved when Sara agreed to have the necessary blood test. Later that night, Esther's cell phone rang. A technician excitedly reported, "It is incredible, it is a perfect match. A match like this is usually only from an immediate blood relative." Elated, Esther immediately called Mrs. Cohen with the great news. That same night, procedures were begun for the transplant to take place.

Two days later, Esther's cell phone rang again. Sara was calling with an invitation to attend her baby's naming. It was to take place at their local synagogue. "You were so kind and friendly, and we know so few people here, won't you please join us at this happy event?" During the conversation, Esther learned that Sara had recently lost both parents in a tragic automobile accident in South Africa, and that painful memory was one of the reasons they had left the country. Esther happily agreed to come to the baby naming. Later that day, Esther told Mr. Cohen of the baby naming of the daughter of the bone-marrow donor. "Why don't you join me there. They haven't been in Israel long, and I know the couple would appreciate it if you came." He agreed to attend.

Thursday morning, Esther and Mr. Cohen went to the synagogue for the ceremony. When the baby's name was pronounced, Mr. Cohen turned pale from the shock of hearing that they had named their baby girl Batya. The new parents had no knowledge of the loss of the Cohen's daughter or even that her name had been Batya.

Sara explained to those assembled why she had chosen that name. "I was adopted," she said. "I have always known it, and I have always felt grateful to my birth mother for giving me life and for giving me up for adoption instead of ending the pregnancy. My adoptive mother, who could not conceive a child, often told me that I was a gift to them from G-d. Now that I have my own child, I realize that all children are gifts from G-d. Regardless of who gives birth to us or who raises us, we are all G-d's children. So we named our daughter Batya, meaning Daughter of G-d."

The transplant was a complete success, but who was this perfect match? Mrs. Cohen knew the answer. When she was sixteen, thirty years earlier, and living in South Africa, she had become pregnant. Her parents wanted her to abort, but she would not hear of it. She had insisted that she would deliver a child and then give the baby up for an adoption. An older couple was located who were thrilled to raise this child as their own.

Sara was this child, none other than Mrs. Cohen's own first child. Now her daughter had returned the gift of life to her own mother.

Although the names have been changed, this true story was told to Rishe (Mrs. Avrahom) Deitsch by one of the participants. She recorded it under the title, Connecting the Dots, *in the February 2006 issue of the N'shei Chabad Newsletter where it was read and reported to me by Rivky Klein. When I spoke with Mrs. Deitsch, she graciously agreed to allow its inclusion in this book.*

THE BUTTERFLY

Thelma Waller Greenberg

Estelle Okeon enjoyed a reputation as a sweet, delightful lady. She was attracted to butterflies—often wearing butterfly pins and butterfly designs on her clothing. She told her daughter, Elaine Rosenberg, that butterflies reminded her of her own mother who spoke lovingly of the creatures. Whenever she saw a butterfly, Estelle had felt a connection.

Elaine attended a funeral last week in Memphis. It was held at the Baron Hirsch Cemetery where Estelle is buried. It was a beautiful, sunny day, and as Elaine walked past her mother's gravesite that quiet afternoon, she softly said," Hello Mom." At that moment, a pretty butterfly landed on her shoulder. When people standing near Elaine noticed the butterfly, it flew away, but it returned three times, always landing on the same spot of her shoulder.

THE MOTORCYCLE

Warren Brashear

"In 1972 at age twenty-one, my father died in a boating accident," said Warren Brashear. "Since I was only one and a-half at the time, I never knew him."

"Recently, I bought a 1969 Triumph motorcycle. When I told my uncle, he asked, "Did you know your father once bought a 1969 Triumph motorcycle?"

"No, I didn't. No one ever mentioned that to me."

"What color is your cycle?" asked my uncle Bruce Brashear, my father's brother.

"It's burnt orange with grey stripes," I responded.

"That was the color of your Dad's motorcycle!" Bruce exclaimed. "The reason I vividly remember these details," he remarked, "is that your Dad taught me to ride a motorcycle on the one he had bought. He later sold it and used the money to buy the boat in which he drowned."

THE SIGN

William Samuels

While tidying the library at the Memphis Jewish Family Service, my son, who is a social worker with the agency, noticed a heavy metal sign perched against the bookcase.

"The corner area of the room had been dedicated as the Amputee Support Library," he said. "A meeting was scheduled to take place that evening—the first opportunity to show off the library. As I reached to remove the metal sign, its inscription shocked me. It reads:

A Living Garden
In Memory of
Mary and Jake Shine
June 1986.

Today is September 21, 2004. It is a time between Rosh Hashanah and Yom Kippur when many Jews visit the graves of loved ones. Why, I wonder, was I destined to discover this sign today—a sign that was dedicated to my grandparents?"

William Samuels and his wife, Sheryl are remarkable. Subsequent to suffering a devastating automobile accident resulting in the amputation of Sheryl's leg, they established a local organization called Out On A Limb which lends support to all who have sustained loss of limbs.
As she was being taken to surgery for the removal of her leg, I asked Sherri about her state of mind. "I believe in the purposefulness of life," she said. "I believe there is a reason for everything that happens. I do not know why this is happening to me unless it is to enable me to be of greater support to others who suffer great stress."

JOY

Pam Frenzel

We recently met Mrs. Pam Frenzel in Indianapolis. She told us the following story:

"About a month after my nine-year old son Tyler died, I went to lunch with some friends including my next-door neighbor, Dee Bloom. During much of our lunch we talked about Tyler and how much he meant to us." Dee, who was very close to Tyler, was especially devastated over our loss. She remarked, "I wonder when I will get my joy back?"

"After we returned home, there was a knock at my door. I opened it and found Dee, standing with mail in her hand and a strange look on her face."

"I just received this letter from my old high school friend," she said. "We haven't written to each other for years." Handing the opened letter to me she said, "Look at this."

In the letter was a small stone on which was engraved the word "Joy."

GRADE "A"

Lara Shwer

Having tried unsuccessfully for years to have a child, Brian and Lara opted for in-vitro fertilization. It is a very long and involved procedure requiring shots and medication. The embryos are carefully watched from the initial fertilization. They are then graded "A," "B," or "C" Only the "A's" are kept for implantation as they would have the best chance for implementation and pregnancy.

On January 10, 1997, the couple was told to come to Nashville, where the procedure was to be done. The weather was clear when they left their home in Memphis, but it soon began to snow. When they reached Jackson—still 130 miles from Nashville—the snow was falling so heavily the state police closed the highway.

"Please allow us to continue," they pleaded with the state patrolman. "It's critical that we get to Nashville if our procedure is to be successful."

"All right," the compassionate officer said reluctantly, "but be very careful. Driving under these conditions can be extremely hazardous."

The couple inched their way eastward, but prior to reaching their destination they were forced to stop for the night. They were in constant touch with a nurse at the hospital who told them, "We will perform the implantation early in the morning, but it cannot be done later."

Arriving at the hospital after twenty-four emotionally filled hours, many of which were spent in prayer, they were met by a smiling nurse. "How fortunate you are that your arrival was delayed," she exclaimed. "Only one of the embryos was an "A" while the others were "B's". During the night, they became "A's.""

After Mrs. Shwer told me this story, she introduced me to her twin son and daughter. Beaming, she proudly announced, "These are my 'A's!"
Sometime when things don't go according to plan, our lives are guided by a better plan.

THE BUGGY RIDE

Deanna Paul Burson

Mrs. Mable Paul took her daughter, Deanna, and her son, Tommy, to Montreal in 1960 to visit family. She hired the driver of a horse and buggy at the hotel to show her children the old part of the city.

"Would you mind driving a few blocks from your usual route?" she requested the driver. "I'd like to show my children where their grandfather's business was located." The gentleman agreed. As they proceeded down a street, Mrs. Paul said, "Across the street is where his store was located, but there are completely different stores now."

The driver turned around and asked, "Are you talking about David Bloomfield's jewelry store?"

"How on earth did you know?" Mable inquired. "I never mentioned his name or the type of things he sold."

The driver smiled and replied, "My sister worked for your father. I bought this watch from him fifty years ago."

The Bloomfield family has been responsible for several significant gifts to the state of Israel including the following in Jerusalem: the library at Hebrew University, the city's famous soccer stadium, and the lovely floral garden and park near the King David Hotel.

THE BLIND DATE

Joel Braverman

Joel was vacationing in Aspen, Colorado. He had taken a date to dinner, and he was sitting at the bar waiting for her to return from the ladies room. Suddenly he felt a tap on his shoulder. When he turned to see who it was, the attractive young lady apologized. "I am sorry. I thought you were my date, Adam."

Soon they were joined by their respective dates.

"Where are you from?" Joel asked Adam.

"I'm from Lebanon, Pennsylvania," he responded.

"I have a relative there," said Joel. "Do you know Reuben Grosky?"

"He's my cousin," exclaimed Adam.

"He's my grandfather!" proclaimed Joel.

The newly discovered cousins, Joel and Adam, quickly became friends.

THE ADOPTION

Harry Samuels

In a previous story titled, "A Jar of Quarters," we met Marilyn Lipman. She had just shared a compelling story and was leaving Memphis for the airport and her return journey to New York City. As she stood to leave for the airport, she turned to me and declared, "I've only had one coincidence happen to me in my life." (I didn't have time to explain that there was no such thing as coincidence, but rather encouraged her to explain her remark.) "Tell me about it," I said.

"Before moving to Gramercy Park in New York City," she began, "We lived in a house in Hurley, New York. When our next-door neighbor learned that I had previously lived in Memphis, she told me that her nephew and his wife adopted two children who came through an agency in Memphis. I met them years ago when they came to Hurley for a visit." Marilyn didn't mention their names, the name of the family or the agency in Memphis that handled the adoption.

"I realize you're in a hurry to drive to the airport," I replied, "But I'd appreciate it if you'd sit down."

"I don't have much time," she replied.

"Please humor me," I added. "If you aren't sitting down I'm afraid you might fall down after hearing what I have to say. I'll cut to the bottom line and will fill you in on the details later if you're interested. When it came time for that couple to receive their son and daughter, I'm the one who handed each child to them!"

This story began in St. Louis, Missouri, shortly after World War II. It concerns a remarkable couple, Sam and Lee Krupnick. They were highly regarded as role models of the city. Sam served as president of numerous non-profit organizations and was an advisor to several presidents of the United States. They were close friends of my sister and brother-in-law, Rose and Alfred Frager.

Unable to have children, the Krupnicks applied to adopt Susan, a refugee from Germany. I remember meeting Susan the first week she arrived. Lee Krupnick took us to her bedroom and pointed under her bed. There were canned goods, vegetables and fruit the little girl had hidden—a vestige of the hunger she had experienced in Europe. Susan had initially been sent to an adoption agency in Memphis but was subsequently transferred to a sister agency in St. Louis. Prior to the completion of the adoption process and contrary to established rules, Susan was placed with the Krupnicks. In the interim, a relative surfaced in Memphis. Jack Lieberman, the executive of the Memphis agency, was compelled to file a lawsuit to recover control of the child on behalf of the newly discovered relative. "It was a very painful experience," he confided," It was like filing a lawsuit against G-d, but prior to the trial, the case was settled and Susan was legally adopted by the Krupnicks."

Susan had a wonderful childhood with Sam and Lee and became a close friend of my niece, Maris Frager, who was married at the Krupnick home.

While speaking with my sister, years later, she indicated that the Krupnicks were very distraught. She told me that Susan and her husband could not have children, and they had not been able to adopt.

Since I was friendly with Mr. Lieberman, who still directed the adoption agency, I called the Krupnicks and offered to be of help. They urged me to do anything possible to help them obtain a grandchild. The following day I made an appointment to see Mr. Lieberman. As I entered his office, I asked his secretary to hold his calls and began our conversation by asking," Do you remember the Susan Krupnick case?"

He turned pale, explaining that the filing of that lawsuit was the most painful experience of his career.

"How would you like to see this come full circle?" I offered.

Six months later I received a call from Susan advising me that she and her husband were coming to Memphis to collect their son. As the intermediary between the foster parent and the adoptive couple, I was the one who brought the baby to them at the offices of the adoption agency. Two years later, I handed them a daughter.

When I finished providing this background information, Marilyn Lipman thanked me for insisting that she be seated." If not, I would have probably fainted," she said.

THE DONOR

Marilyn Bozoff Zellner

Stanley Shipowitz lives in Virginia Beach, Virginia. When Stan's diabetes forced him to seek a kidney donor, things looked pretty bleak. It is very difficult to obtain an organ through the national registry—especially if the recipient is in his mid-60s. He began looking desperately for a living donor.

"Dad," his son Louis announced," I want to be tested as a prospective donor."

"Son, I appreciate your willingness to help, but since you were adopted, the chances of being a match for me would be infinitesimal."

"I still want to try. Please let me be tested," Louis insisted.

When the results were obtained, it was found that he was a perfect match. Last year the procedure was performed successfully.

THE GUEST BOOK

Shelley Smuckler

Lori Smuckler lived in Chicago. Her roommate had just advised her that she would be leaving the city and would not renew the lease on their apartment. The lease was to expire September 1, and Lori only had two weeks to find another roommate or move to a less desirable efficiency far away from the "Gold Coast."

A few days before the deadline, Lori received a telephone call from a lady in Philadelphia in response to her newspaper advertisement. Lori asked, "Where are you from originally?" The lady responded, "St. Louis, Missouri." "So am I," Lori told her. "What's your last name?" "Abrams," she answered.

Lori called her parents to see if they or her sister, Julie, knew the family, but no one did. Shelley insisted that her daughter could not commit for a year's lease with someone who was unknown to them. She planned to drive to Chicago to help her move to another apartment prior to the deadline.

The following day Shelley was house shopping in St. Louis with her daughter, Julie. They had looked at numerous houses in the western suburbs when Julie said, "Mom, there's a quicker way back if you take the other street." As they drove the new route, they spotted a subdivision with its model house sign. "As long as we're here why don't we see what they have to offer?" Julie suggested.

They began examining the model house. The salesman, who was helping a middle-aged couple, emphatically insisted that everyone sign the guest book.

Shelley started to sign the book when she noticed the name of the couple that had just left. She abruptly ran outside to speak with them. "You'll never guess who I am," she announced. "My name is Shelley Smuckler and your daughter is planning to lease an apartment in Chicago with my daughter, Lori."

"I am so happy we were able to meet each other," Mrs. Abrams declared. "Your daughter gave my daughter your telephone number, but my husband and I were reluctant to call. What could we say? 'Is your daughter nice?' The salesman in this model was so pushy, I almost wrote a fictitious name in his book. Had I done so, we would have never met."

PART II
LOVE STORIES

HERMAN AND ROMA

Harry Samuels

Last year a friend sent a newspaper article telling of a *bar mitzvah* that was held sixty-three years late for Herman Rosenblatt. When I spoke with Herman, he was very cordial and told the following story that he felt would fit nicely into *Crossroads*.

"Herman," his friend, Sid, said, "I have a date this weekend. She has a really cute girl friend named Roma who is a nurse who speaks Polish. Why don't you call her and we'll double date. I can give you her telephone number if you're interested."

He wasn't interested in a blind date, but Sid kept pestering and a date was arranged.

Herman and Roma immediately felt a special attraction to each other. He had seriously dated several others, but for some reason, he decided that none of them were meant for him. He and Roma spoke of their past. He told her that he had been born and reared in Poland and had come to America after being liberated from a concentration camp following World War ll.

"I served in the American army and once traveled to Israel on a visit," he said.

"That's remarkable," she offered. "I served as a nurse in Israel after I left Poland, and I believe I once met someone in Israel who looked very much like you." The two continued to exchange details until they had established the fact that they had indeed met while in Israel. As their conversation continued he asked Roma, "How did you spend the war years?"

"A Catholic priest arranged for my family to live on a farm near a concentration camp named Schlieben. It was located close to Dresden. I was ten and remember throwing apples over an electrified fence to a thirteen year-old boy. I would wait until the guard wasn't watching—he would have shot us had he caught us. I often wonder if that boy survived the war."

Tears of joy began streaming down Herman's face. "Do you remember that boy telling you that he was leaving Schlieben the next day and that you shouldn't return?"

"How did you know?" she stammered.

"It was me," he sobbed, "I was that boy and I am not going to lose you again!" That evening he proposed. They have been married forty-nine years.

At age ten Herman Rosenblatt was taken to the first of several concentration camps with his parents and three brothers. His parents died in the camps, and he often felt they were the lucky ones. The Nazi guards gave him the job of hauling victims from the gas chambers to the crematorium. They treated him brutally, once beating him so severely that he was blinded for several days. He was starving when he met Roma and received her apples.

After his story appeared on CBS and NBC television in Long Island, a local rabbi held a bar mitzvah ceremony for him—sixty-three years late. "I spoke with that rabbi recently," Herman told me. "He said that the attendance at his synagogue has increased twenty-five percent since my bar mitzvah!"

FINDING THEIR BESHERT

Harry Samuels

One definition of the word *beshert* is soul mate or life partner ...

Rabbi Shlomo Riskin had made a tremendous impact on the Lincoln Square Synagogue located in the upper west side of New York City. He arranged to accompany a group of young singles to Israel. He wanted to show them the country and to share that unique experience with them. Prior to the trip, he organized the participants into groups based upon their level of religious commitment. Although he was observant, he wanted everyone to feel comfortable so as not to impose more traditional schedules on those who would not be interested.

As he stood behind the table assigning the more committed travelers to their appropriate bus, a lovely young lady approached. "Are you observant?" He inquired.

She replied, "Of course I am," responding to the question in a secular, not a religious context—meaning: "I notice things around me." "And that," said Rabbi Riskin, "is how I met my *beshert*."

While at the Lincoln Square Synagogue which was known for its outreach to the unaffiliated, Rabbi Riskin increased membership from 200 to several thousand. He established a network of high schools for young men and women, which has developed into the Ohr Torah Stone network of high schools, colleges, graduate programs, seminaries, and rabbinical schools in Israel with current membership exceeding 4,000. When he left to serve as rabbi of the city of Efrat, Israel, over seventy families from New York joined him and his family.

When I spoke with him in Memphis last year, he shared another interesting anecdote. His son was serving in the Israeli army. The unit was so highly classified that all of the mail was censored. The censor was a young, single lady who was impressed with the beautiful poetry included in young Riskin's letters. She decided to write him a letter, and they began a correspondence that ultimately led to their marriage.

THE PHOTOGRAPH

Irma Sheon

Romaine and David, who met on a blind date in June of 2003, were immediately drawn to each other. They each initially felt a strong connection, fell deeply in love, and were engaged within nine months. They later discovered that their connection dated back to 1954, over ten years before either of them was born.

When visiting his mother, Janet, David remarked that she bore a striking resemblance to photos he had seen of Romaine's mother who had passed away when Romaine was nine years old. This remark triggered Janet's memory. She began searching through her old letters and memorabilia, and she produced a newspaper clipping a friend had sent her in 1954. It was an article about someone neither she nor her friend knew. But because it included a photograph of a woman to whom she had such an uncanny resemblance, Janet kept it for fifty years. That woman was Romaine's mother who had been married to David Mountbatten of British royalty, prior to her marriage with James Orthwein, Romaine's father.

The idea that David's mother had been in possession of a photograph of Romaine's mother since 1954, continues to amaze the bride and groom and their families."

My cousin, Irma Sheon, alerted me to this story that had been reported in the Sunday edition of the New York Times on December 12, 2004. I called the newlyweds, David and Romaine Gutterman, who graciously granted permission to use their story. It seemed very unlikely that I would have had any relationship with these people, yet during our conversations; it became apparent that we too were connected in several ways.

"Do you know Jim and Judy Lindy from Memphis?" David asked." Yes," I replied. "I know them well. Why do you ask?"
"Their daughter, Phyllis, married my brother," he answered.

When I entered college in 1948, I had become friendly with Patricia Busch, a relative of Romaine's. I have never met Romaine's father, but we had at least two mutual acquaintances.

"David, do you know if your paternal grandfather came from Russia?" I asked. "I have a feeling you were named after him and that his first name was Dovid."
"I believe he came from Kiev," he answered. "Why do you ask?"
"My maternal grandfather also came from Kiev, and his name was Dovid Gutterman!"

GOOD ADVICE

Rabbi Chaim Mentz

In the summer of 2004, Andrew and Sharon became engaged and asked me to officiate at their wedding on December 5th. I listed the basic requirements that must be fulfilled for an orthodox ceremony. One of these requirements is that a get (Jewish divorce) must be obtained if either partner had been married previously to a Jewish person and had not dissolved the marriage in accordance with Jewish law.

During a private conversation, Sharon confided that she was once married to a Jewish man for six hours. She referred to him as "the mistake." The courts granted her an annulment immediately due to the terrible actions of "the mistake."

I could feel knots forming in my stomach. How do I tell her the last thing on earth she wants to hear? I began by saying that whether it is six hours or six years, it is still considered as a marriage.

"But the courts annulled my marriage! Rabbi, please understand. It was a mistake." She couldn't believe what I said. "I told her, I really want to do your wedding. Please understand I can't do it until you obtain a Jewish divorce."

"What if I can't find the 'mistake? Am I doomed forever?"

"Let's not speculate," I said. "I will contact the Jewish courts in Los Angeles who will help us resolve this dilemma." I explained to both Sharon and Andrew that nothing happens without a reason. The fact that you need a *get* today shows that something important happened in Sharon's life, even if it only lasted six hours.

Sharon would not allow her wedding to be stopped due to her "mistake." She continued to plan her wedding and honeymoon. After spending weeks with the Jewish courts in Los Angeles, Sharon was finally freed. However the courts told her, "You cannot marry before ninety-two days from today."

"What do they mean?" the couple asked. "Are they crazy? Is this true? Will you not marry us on December 5 as we had planned?"

I calmly explained the Jewish law,—why there is a ninety-two-day waiting period—and I tried to reason with them. All they could think about was their wedding plans and their honeymoon. They just couldn't understand why they would have to wait an additional month.

A few days later they called to say they wished to be married in accordance with Jewish law, and they rescheduled the wedding until the end of January. Still in the back of their minds they couldn't understand why G-d was delaying their wedding—not until December 26. That was the time when Andrew and Sharon were supposed to be on the last few days of their honeymoon. They had been scheduled to stay at the famous Kaafu Atoll Maldives hotel on Lankanfushi Island. Had they been there at that time, their hotel room would have been swept away by the tsunami.

Rabbi Mentz granted permission for including this remarkable story.

THE BOYFRIEND

Sharon Tabachnick

"As a young woman living in Kyriat Gat, Israel, I fell in love with a boy named Eli who lived in Tel Aviv. We had wonderful times together, but it became apparent that he had no plans to marry, and although it was a tough decision, I ended our relationship.

A few years later, I met another young man with whom I fell in love. His name was Stephen, but he was called by his middle name, Ely. It seemed strange that the two loves of my life would share the same name albeit spelled differently.

Ely and I soon decided to marry. I loved him very much but wanted to be sure I didn't still love Eli. I prayed for a chance to see Eli one more time before my marriage to help me decide if I was making the right decision. Shortly thereafter, I went to Beersheba, where Ely lived, to discuss our wedding plans. We both loved sunflower seeds and peanuts, and we went to the Central Bus Station where they sold the best in town.

I remember that evening clearly. The normally busy station was almost deserted—eerily so—as we sat on a bench munching nuts. Soon a young man appeared. It was Eli who had traveled from Tel Aviv to Beersheba to meet someone. Why he was there at that specific day and time when the station was almost deserted, enabling us to easily spot each other, seemed very mysterious.

I introduced Eli to Ely and mentioned our upcoming marriage. Eli was very polite and congratulated us. There seemed to be some regret in his voice, but afterwards I was convinced that I was doing the right thing. I realized that only the hand of G-d could have arranged for all of the things to be in place so that we could meet one more time as I had so fervently prayed.

Ely and I have now been married thirty years, and that night in Beersheba was the last time I saw Eli."

NIGHT

Dr. David Patterson

Dr. David Patterson graciously gave the following to me in response to my request for a story. As you will see, his life and the lives of countless others have been positively impacted by the gift of a book:

"In the fall of 1979, while I was teaching at the University of Oregon, a student named Matthew came into my office cradling four books in his arms. In the course of long conversations on life and the meaning of life, I had recommended to him a number of books, and he had studiously read them all. Now he offered me something to read, and I could not refuse his offering. I scanned the titles: *Night, Dawn, The Accident*, and *The Town Beyond the Wall*—Elie Wiesel's first four books. Gently placing the volumes on my desk, he said,' you must read these, but read this one first. *Night*.'(The most read book on the Holocaust—an autobiography of the author's experiences in the Buchenwald concentration camp.) I ran my fingers over the binding of the book he handed me. It felt unusually warm, and the memory of that feeling came back to me when later I noticed on the back of one of the volumes the statement, 'To read Wiesel is to burn with him.'"

"Two years passed. I was still reading and re-reading, pouring over everything that Wiesel had published—as I still do—digging for the fire in those ashes, wrestling the light from that darkness. And, like Jacob at Peniel, I wrestled with my own soul. Every volume, every page, every silence between words, made me into something other, destroying me and raising me up again.

During the fall of 1981, it struck me that this man, whose words I had been blessed to receive, was still alive. So many others who had confronted me with life-threatening and therefore life-enhancing collisions were gone—Pascal, Kierkegaard, Dostoevsky, Buber, and the others. All had passed from this world, but he was still alive. Fearing even then it might be too late, I hurriedly wrote him a brief letter in an attempt to say what he had meant to me, what he had taught me, while there was still time—trying to express my gratitude for his testimony.

After two years of correspondence, I looked forward to my first visit to see Professor Wiesel. He cordially invited me into his apartment, and we began a dialogue that enabled me to delve deeper into his world. I began by asking, 'How do you deal with the prospect of perhaps being the last one to remember?' He responded in soft-spoken yet powerful tones, and I listened. It was the beginning of a friendship that has lasted until this day."

"Two years later as a professor of Russian and East European Literature at Oklahoma State University, I was teaching my first course on the Holocaust in addition to a seminar on Eli Wiesel. That evening there was to be a lecture by some guy named Gerri Alperin of the Anti-Defamation League office in Dallas, and I decided to check him out.

He turned out to be a she. I was transfixed. Her lecture was as brilliant as she was beautiful.

I wanted to talk to her further about what she had said concerning the Holocaust, and I wanted to get to know her. The next morning Gerri and I met for breakfast to discuss Holocaust education, texts important to studying this vast topic, resource materials, and more. It was all very professional—mostly professional. Within a month I was spending my weekends in Dallas.

The first time I entered her apartment, the thousands of books that lined her bookshelves mesmerized me. She had approximately two thousand books on the Holocaust and another two thousand books on Judaica. It was a priceless treasure, a unique collection rivaling almost any university library's collection. I could think of no better dowry. Somehow I convinced her to be my wife, and within six months of our meeting we were married.

I started reading these thousands of books, and I started writing. I had written on other subjects, but now I had a sense of mission that possessed me. Based on what my beautiful wife had brought me—based on the holiness of our marital union—I entered into an encounter with the most profound questions of good and evil, G-d and humanity that have shaped the millennial history of the Jewish people. With her there came to me a calling that I could not refuse. I did not choose, it chose me: my student Matthew, my friendship with Elie Wiesel, my marriage to Gerri, my writing—an attempt to give voice to the Six Million whose voices were silenced—all has led to a time and place and the realization that it was all *beshert*."

Dr. David Patterson heads the Bornblum Judaic Studies Program at the University of Memphis. He is the author of twenty-seven books including thirteen on the Holocaust. Additionally, he has co-authored with Elie Wiesel: In Dialogue and Dilemma: Conversations with Elie Wiesel.

PART III
TRAVELS

VIENNA REVISITED

Harry Samuels

In *Beshert: True Stories of Connections* I told of our bizarre experience while traveling in Vienna during May 2004. Prior to leaving Memphis, I asked for the names of Lubavitcher rabbis living in Vienna. Since I speak Yiddish, their first language, I knew I could communicate with them in case a problem arose. I was given three names.

On our last day in Vienna, we decided to locate those men and visit their synagogue. We wanted to learn of the experience of people living as Jews in that city of 1,700,000 where Hitler had lived and where the Nazis had reduced the Jewish population from 185,000 in 1938 to only 15,000 today. We questioned several people on the tram, but each gave us different directions—far from our immediate location.

As we crossed a charming bridge spanning a tributary of the Danube River, I suddenly felt a compulsion to walk to the other side. "Something is drawing me across," I announced." It was irrational inasmuch as I had never been there, but my wife and our traveling companions agreed to humor me. We strolled a couple of blocks almost directly to a group of men who were walking along an intersecting street. Two of those three rabbis whose names I had been given were among them.

After speaking with the strangers, we continued walking and subsequently discovered the site of the former Leopoldstadt Synagogue, the largest temple in Vienna that had been destroyed during Kristallnacht.

Three months after this experience, we visited the Chautauqua Institution in Chautauqua, New York. My book had not been published, but friends had asked me to bring a copy of its manuscript for a presentation. I set aside a Thursday afternoon to do so and invited fourteen to the public room of our condominium. As I began, I noticed a stranger walking up the stairs to her apartment. "You're welcome to join us," I said.

She sat on a couch near me, but I could sense that her mind was not on the anecdotes. In previous readings, when some of the more dramatic stories are told, the usual responses are: "That gives me chills," or "My arms are covered with goose bumps." Instead the woman, Diane Arch, showed no emotional response. She merely stared into space. Propitiously, Stephanie Rosenblatt arrived. I introduced her to the group as a former citizen of Germany who had survived the Holocaust. "I did not plan to tell the following story of our recent experience in Vienna," I said, "but in your honor I will now do so."

When I mentioned Vienna, Diane's face lit up. As I continued with the story, it became apparent that she was making a connection. When I told of our having found the site of the famous Leopoldstadt Synagogue, she could no longer contain herself. She blurted out: "My grandfather was the president of the synagogue that evening in 1938 when it was destroyed. He saved a Torah scroll, escaped to America, and donated it to a synagogue in Denver, Colorado, where it is still in use."

Later I reminded Diane of her strange demeanor that afternoon, She replied, "I had just returned from a lecture at the Hall of Philosophy. I had heard a talk given by someone who had been an interpreter at the Nuremberg Trials. My family had lived in Vienna, and many were killed. As you began speaking, I was still recalling the horror of those times."

LAS VEGAS

Harry Samuels

Earlier last year, we flew to Las Vegas to see the new hotels there. Flora and I sat in a three-seat row with a friendly young man named Brad. We quickly became acquainted.

"Where are you from? I asked.

"Pittsburgh," he replied. "I'm a Methodist youth minister there."

"Are you going to Las Vegas to learn about the devil?" I teased.

"No," he answered, "Tomorrow is Valentine's Day, and I thought it would be neat if I visited my girl friend, Linda. I only have twenty-six hours before returning home, and I'm really excited about the prospect of seeing her. She's at the University of Nevada, working on her Ph.D. in psychology, and she doesn't know I'm coming. Several of our friends are taking her on a scavenger hunt. They've arranged the final clue to take them at noon to a restaurant at the Paris Hotel on the Las Vegas Strip, She doesn't realize the prize for solving the last puzzle is going to be ME!"

We were intrigued with the prospect of meeting his girl friend. We told him we would see them at noon the next day and take a picture of the occasion.

The following morning we visited New York, New York and some of the other hotels. As time passed, we dismissed the idea of seeing Brad and Linda since we were far away from the site of their planned meeting. Instead we began walking through the cavernous MGM Grand Hotel. Eventually we approached a large glass enclosure where lions are often displayed. There, standing alone before us was Brad, smiling profusely.

"I changed our meeting place since this was closer," he said, "I walked the Strip hoping to see you and advise you of the change of plans, but with so many people here, it was impossible to find you." At that moment, Linda arrived, and we captured the moment with a picture of the couple.

Brad has advised us that he is planning to present stories from my first book to the teenagers in his ministry. He also said we would be invited to his wedding.

ITALY

Marilyn & Sam Fox

Jeff and Greg are sons of our good friends Marilyn and Sam Fox of St. Louis, Missouri, who provided the following:

During the 80s, Jeff and Greg were traveling in Europe on an Italian train. The passenger car to which they were assigned became extremely crowded. Jeff decided they should move. "Why don't we go to another car that's less crowded," he said. "I don't care if we were assigned here. At least we'll be able to rest."

Later their parents received a call from the boys. "Our train was in a terrible accident," they announced. "The passenger car we had just left was completely destroyed."

During that trip, the two boys were sitting in a plaza in Florence, Italy. They were enjoying lunch near the Uffizi art museum when they were startled by the sound of someone revving a motorcycle. Before they could protest the unwelcome racket, they noticed the driver, who seemed oblivious to them. It was their brother, Steve, who had been traveling alone throughout Europe that summer. He had not been in touch with his siblings and was unaware of their location.

A book should be written about Sam and Marilyn Fox. The three of us attended Washington University together, and Sam and I were fraternity brothers. He came to St. Louis from Desloge, Missouri, in 1947, and has made an enormous impact on society—locally, nationally and internationally. He is the founder, chairman, and chief executive officer of a private firm, the Harbor Group, Ltd., operating one hundred forty companies worldwide with twelve thousand employees. He and Marilyn have served numerous charitable organizations as financial supporters and in leadership positions. Sam has been especially devoted to Washington University where most recently he has been responsible for a dramatic expansion of its endowment fund. He is life trustee and former vice chairman of its board.

For sixty years I have been seeking someone who had a connection with my father's hometown in Poland. Its population was minuscule, and I had given up the idea of learning much about it. Recently, Sam heard me mention its name, Annapol. "That's where my mother lived," he told me. "We took a film crew there and have several hours of unedited tape of our visit."

THE CRUISE

Gina Sugarmon

Judge Russell Sugarmon, a dynamic and personable African-American from Memphis, is a graduate of Harvard Law School, perhaps the most prestigious in America. He met and developed a friendship with Marvin Ratner, a successful, white, Jewish attorney. They joined forces and established the first integrated law practice in Memphis and the south in July 1967.

Marvin became a specialist in estate planning; Russell became a general sessions court judge. The two men remained close friends, as did their wives, Gina and Sara.

The Sugarmons and Ratners had planned a cruise when Marvin died on December 1, 2000. Since they had already paid for the trip, Russell and Gina opted to take the cruise with another couple on a newly commissioned ship.

During the cruise Gina would often look wistfully at the balcony of their neighbor's suite—the one Marvin and Sara were to have had—and she remarked how nice it would have been had their friends been there.

On the last night, as they walked into the dining room for the gala dinner, Gina felt drawn to a tripod containing pictures. One picture stood out so prominently it seemed to shout—"look here, we've been with you during this entire cruise!" It was a picture of Marvin and Sara that had obviously been taken on a previous trip.

MONTREAL

Harry Samuels

While on a trip to Montreal, Canada, in 1988, my wife Flora insisted on sending picture post cards to some friends. The cards she selected from the drugstore were completely black on the front side except for the caption that read, "Montréal At Night." The message Flora wrote on the other side read, "Wish you could see Montreal."

"This is so silly," I chided. "Why not send some of these other cards with scenes of the city?" But she was adamant in her selection, and the cards were mailed.

During the night, a snowstorm in Newfoundland caused the electric transmission lines to collapse. Since they supplied most of the electric power to Ontario and a large portion of the northeastern United States, it caused a complete blackout. The incident was widely reported in all of the major newspapers in the country—the day the cards arrived.

FLIGHT 847

Aarron & Sue Balkin

Returning from a trip to the Greek Islands, Aaron "Bud" and Sue Balkin waited patiently in the Athens airport. Their flight to New York had been delayed due to engine problems, and they tried to convince the clerk to allow them to switch to TWA flight 847.

"Please let us switch our flight," Sue implored. "Our luggage has already been loaded on the other airplane, but we'll bring it to you if you'll just hold the flight for us."

They rushed as quickly as they could, but, alas, the flight left without them.

"What rotten luck," they agreed." It wouldn't have hurt them to wait a few minutes for us."

As flight 847 left for Rome and Boston that 15th day of June 1985, it was hijacked by Arab gunmen. They forced the pilot to fly to Beirut, Lebanon, and then to Algiers, Morocco. There were 104 Americans among the 145 passengers. The hijackers beat several Americans and killed a U.S. Marine.

Sometimes we are fortunate when our wishes are not granted.

THE JUDGE

Harry Samuels

We had traveled to Lake Worth, Florida, to visit with our friends, Edward and Barbara Feldman. After dinner we went to a movie in a small, nearby theater. The room was well lit, and there were only ten or twelve couples present. Before the movie started, the Feldmans introduced us to the couple seated directly in front of my wife and me. "These are our next door neighbors," they said. "Where are you from?" I asked them. "I'm originally from Bergen County, New Jersey," the lady replied.

"I have friends who lived in Tenafly. Have you ever heard of Harvey Sorkow?"

"His parents were neighbors of my parents," she replied.

Another couple overheard this exchange. They questioned us in a doubting manner, "What is his wife's name?" "Pearl," I answered.

They couldn't wait to tell us that the Sorkows had just spent ten days as their houseguests in Florida.

We were staying at a hotel in West Palm Beach that week. After being treated exceptionally well by the manager, I asked where he was from. "I live near Hackensack, New Jersey," he said.

"That's where my friend Harvey Sorkow worked," I noted. "Have you ever heard of him?"

"He was a friend of my uncle who also served as a judge in Hackensack. I remember being introduced to him years ago," he replied.

A few months following the above two incidents, I received a telephone call from Stan and Tamar Rabin who live in Rockville, Maryland. They belong to a book club to which I had spoken months earlier.

"You'll never believe what happened to us a few weeks ago," Stan declared. "We were visiting an art gallery in La Jolla, California, when Tamar saw an old friend and her husband who were with another couple. During lunch, Tamar's friend declared, "Meeting you here after so many years was *beshert*,"

Stan replied, "We just read a book by that title, and we heard a presentation by its author."

"Do you mean Harry Samuels?" Asked the other couple.

"How do you know him?" Tamar questioned.

"He was my fraternity brother at college," answered Harvey Sorkow.

Harvey Sorkow became a distinguished judge in Hackensack, New Jersey. One of his decisions made headlines in newspapers across the country. It was the first surrogate mother case—known as the Baby M *case.*

The Sorkow's daughter, Janice, shared an interesting experience. She traveled to Boston in 1976. On the four-hour drive from Boston to her home in New Jersey, she lost a distinctive gold earring. Last year she found it in a jewelry case at a thrift store in Newton, Mass.

MISTAKEN IDENTITY

Theo Garb

As a gregarious individual, Theo Garb makes friends easily. While sailing on a ship from Ireland to the United States in 1950, he was seated for dinner next to Mr. Spiro. Quickly, they determined that they had numerous connections with each other.

"Your grandfather was a friend of ours," Mr. Spiro acknowledged. "I remember vividly the times I rode with him in Europe on his sleigh." For the entire cruise, Mr. Garb and Mr. Spiro were inseparable. They vowed to remain friends, but after arriving in the United States, they lost track of each other.

Twenty years later, while traveling on a train from Paris to Switzerland, Theo glanced through a window in a compartment of the train and saw a familiar face. When its occupant came to the door, Theo hugged him. "I am so happy to see you," Theo said, "after such a long time, it seems strange to meet you here."

"Do I know you? The man asked.

"Your name is Spiro, isn't it?" Theo insisted.

"Yes, but how did you know?" he questioned.

Theo asserted, "I either know you or your twin."

"Of course, that's the answer," the man affirmed. "I'm a twin."

THE BEGGAR

Maryland Science Center

Miss Bridget McDermott, age twenty-eight, was one of fourteen traveling from County Mayo to visit her cousins in St. Louis, Missouri.

The night before she departed, Bridget gave a few coins to a beggar. He took the money and told her that she was about to go on a long journey. "There will be a tragedy, but you will be saved," the man said.

The date: April 11, 1912
The place of embarkation: Queenstown, England.
The line: The White Star
The ship: The Titanic

Bridgett traveled third class, which meant four to a room, far below deck. The chances for survival of those in this category were minuscule, however, as predicted by the beggar, she was saved.

DELAYED MEETING

Gene Camerik

Gene Camerik served in the United States Navy. In 1953, his ship was docked in France. "My shipmate Elmer Anderson and I decided to explore Paris," he explained. "As we approached the *Arc de Triomphe,* a man standing nearby overheard our conversation. He was dressed in a business suit and was selling nightclub tours to passersby. In our U.S. Navy uniforms, we looked like fair game, and as an icebreaker he asked us in English where in the United States we were from. That was our first clue that he was an American."

"I'm from Norfolk, Virginia and my friend, Mr. Anderson, hails from Burbank, California," I replied.

"I used to date a girl from Burbank," the man stated. "Her name was Susan Anderson. Did you ever hear of her?"

"She's my sister," answered my friend.

"Is your name Elmer Anderson by any chance?" The stranger queried.

"How did you know?"

"Susan mentioned you often and wanted to introduce us, but you always stayed out so late we never got together. We had to come to Paris to meet!"

Gene Camerik is the author of Black Night Bright Dawn. *New York: I Universe, 2003,*

PART IV
RIPPLES

BOB

Harry Samuels

Last year we attended the funeral service of a dear friend, Robert Y. Fleming. During the eulogy at Second Presbyterian Church, the minister spoke of Bob's ability to develop friendships quickly with a wide range of individuals.

"Bob had been diagnosed with lung cancer and was being treated at the West Clinic in Memphis," the minister told the packed assembly. "It was there, he and his wife, Joanne, met and became friendly with Dr. Andrews and his wife, Marjory." Dr. Andrews, who had performed medical missionary work in Kenya, was also undergoing treatment at the clinic. As the two couples were leaving the facility on June 29, Dr. Andrews remarked, "Bob, it was wonderful visiting with you and Joanne today. I'll see you next Wednesday or I will see you in Heaven."

The following day, both men died.

Bob and I had been friends for over fifteen years when we discovered a new connection. I explained that I had served in the U.S. Army during the Korean War and was stationed at Aberdeen Proving Grounds in Maryland. I remarked that I was a corporal when I was assigned to teach Troop Information and Education for the regiment. Captain Eugene C. Fleming was my boss, and he was extremely nice considering the disparity in our ranks. We became friends to the extent that years later, he and his wife visited me in Jonesboro, Arkansas. This is pretty far-fetched, I told Bob, "But do you know someone named Eugene C. Fleming, Jr., who lived in West Virginia?"
Bob smiled, "He's my cousin, and he's named after my father!"

YOUNG FRIEND

Alvin Malnik

Sixty-six years ago when my friend Alvin Malnik was a five-year-old, he lived with his parents in a four family apartment house in St. Louis, Missouri. Another family, the Hershkovitzs, lived in one of the apartments. The Hershkovitzs had taken pity on Loebel, a young, homeless, German refugee and had brought him to America to live with them.

Al reminisced, "I could understand a little Yiddish spoken by my parents, and because of its similarity to the German language, I was able to communicate with Loebel. We became friends, but after a couple of years, he left."

Forty years later, while sitting in the lobby of the Sands Hotel in Las Vegas, Al felt himself strangely drawn to a group of men sitting at a nearby table. Addressing one of the gentlemen he said, "I know you. Your name is Hershkovitz."

"You're mistaken," the man said. "My name is Ponato, and I'm from California."

"I continued to insist that he was my old childhood friend, but he was equally adamant in denying it. Feeling frustrated, I walked away—still convinced that I was right.

A half-hour later, when I went to the men's room, he followed me."

"You were right," the man admitted. "The Hershkovitz couple was unable to keep me. They sent me to an orphanage in California where I was adopted. I'm astonished that you remembered me after such a long time."

Alvin Malnik and I attended Washington University and were fraternity brothers. He has led an interesting life. After becoming an attorney, he established a law practice in Florida. At age twenty-five, he successfully defended Jimmy Hoffa in a trial in which Robert Kennedy was the opposing counsel. During lunch last December in Palm Beach, he shared an anecdote with my wife and me. He asked if we had seen the movie The Aviator, *which was an Academy Award nominee. "Here is something that wasn't in the movie," he told us.*

"I was in my mid-twenties and practicing law in Florida when I received a call from a client." 'We are sending a private plane to bring you to Las Vegas,' *his client began.* 'We would like you to negotiate the sale of the Sands Hotel. We owe ten million dollars on its mortgage and would like to sell it for thirty-seven million. Go to the penthouse of the Desert Inn Hotel at midnight and knock on the door. The rest is up to you.'

"I followed directions and knocked on the door. A voice inside the apartment asked, 'Are you the lawyer?' *"Yes," I replied.*

'How much do you want for the hotel?'

"I was young and inexperienced, and I told him it would be forty-seven million,"

'That is ridiculous, but write it up,' *he replied.* "On what? *I asked.* 'On this,' *he answered, slipping a legal pad under the door.*

The deal was finally made for an acceptable asking price, and that is how the sale of the Sands Hotel was negotiated with Howard Hughes."

DON

Harry Samuels

Standing before my desk in 1961 was a man dressed in a dark blue uniform. He appeared to be an airplane pilot, but he introduced himself as Don Adams, a baggage handler for American Airlines. "I operate a fence company in my spare time," he said, "and I'd like to rent some space in your discount store for my business." He was very persuasive, and we agreed to a lease. We became good friends and his business prospered until he was convinced to include building construction in his operation. Since he was undercapitalized, he was soon forced into bankruptcy. My partner and I suggested he become an insurance salesman with State Farm Insurance Company. He took our advice and was very successful. He developed his agency into one of the best in Memphis.

In the meantime my partner, Vic, and I developed a commercial real estate firm. Following Vic's death, Don insisted I share an office in his suite in order to satisfy the requirements for my commercial real estate license. I only visited the office periodically to collect mail.

One sunny afternoon in July 2003, I remarked to my wife, "I haven't seen Don lately. I believe I'll go to his office." It was 3 p.m. when I arrived, and Don had just left for the day. As I walked into my office I noticed a man sitting at my desk. He was most amiable and introduced himself as Miller Loosier. "After thirty years," he recounted, "I am retiring from a job with State Farm as an administrator. My family and I are moving to Memphis from Cincinnati. My goal is to take over an existing State Farm agency."

Impressed with the gentleman, I suggested, "It's time Don started taking it easy after working so hard most of his life. Why don't you ask if he would be interested in selling this agency?"

Miller smiled, "We just worked out the details and notified the employees. As Don left the office earlier, he turned to me saying, 'I'm so pleased this business we developed is going to be continued by you without any interruption.'"

Miller added that he had not been scheduled to arrive for another month, but he had been required to come early in order to close the loan on their new home.

Early the next morning, I received a telephone call from Geneva Adams, Don's wife.

"How are you doing?" I asked.

"Not so good," she replied. "Don died last night."

THE JEWISH PIRATE

Professor Edward B. Glick

"One of the things I do since I retired from Temple University in 1991 is lecture on cruise ships. My signature talk is the 50-century-old history of piracy, whose practitioners I call the Seafaring Gangsters of the World.

A few weeks before my first gig, I sent a draft of the talk to my history-buff sister, Phyllis. She liked it, but was very unhappy that I had not mentioned Jean Lafitte. She said I simply had to talk about Lafitte because he was unique. He was a Sephardic Jew, as was his first wife who was born in the Danish Virgin Islands.

In his prime, Lafitte ran not just one pirate sloop but also a whole fleet of them simultaneously. He even bought a blacksmith shop in New Orleans, which he used as a front for fencing pirate loot. And he was one of the few buccaneers who didn't die in battle, in prison or on the gallows. Though I didn't lecture about Lafitte at first, a circumstance of serendipity has made me do so ever since.

I was flying to Norfolk, Virginia and began chatting with the man next to me."

"What are you doing on this plane?" he asked.

"My wife and I are picking up a cruise ship in Norfolk."

"Taking a vacation?"

"Not entirely. I'll be giving lectures on the ship each day."

"What do you lecture about?"

"I usually talk about Latin America, the Panama Canal, Portuguese explorations after Prince Henry, the voyages of Captain Cook to the South Pacific and several other topics. But I always begin a cruise with a lecture on pirates. The kids love it, and the old folks like it too."

"Are you going to talk about Jean Lafitte?"

"No," and I repeated what my sister had told me.

"You're going to find this hard to believe, but I am a direct descendant of Jean Lafitte. Your sister is right.

Our family, originally named Lefitto, lived in the Iberian Peninsula for centuries. When Ferdinand and Isabella re-conquered Spain and expelled the Muslims and the Jews in 1492, most of the Jews fled to North Africa. Others went to the Balkans or to Greece and Turkey. But some Sephardic Jews, my ancestors among them, crossed the Pyrenees and settled in France, where Jean was born in about 1780. He moved to French Santo Domingo during the Napoleonic Period. However, a slave rebellion forced him to flee to New Orleans. Eventually, he became a pirate, but he always called himself a privateer because that label has a more legal ring to it.

In 1814, the British sought his aid in their pending attack on New Orleans," he continued, "however, he passed their plans to the Americans and helped General Andrew Jackson beat them in 1815. A grateful Jackson, not yet president, saw to it that Lafitte and his family became American citizens. And by the way, did you know that there's a town of Jean Lafitte, as well as a Jean Lafitte national Historical Park, in southwestern Louisiana?"

"I was flabbergasted, not so much by the saga of Jean Lafitte as retold by a proud descendant, but by the fact that the two of us had met so coincidentally in the skies over Georgia. What is the statistical probability that a descendant of the Franco-Jewish-American pirate Jean Lafitte would board an airplane and sit next to me as I was agonizing over whether to mention his famous ancestor in a forthcoming talk?"

I am grateful to Professor Glick for permission to include this story. He is Emeritus Professor of Political Science at Temple University in Philadelphia where he specialized in Middle East politics, Latin American political culture and the politics of national defense. He has published seven books and is a favorite lecturer on cruise ships.
A friend initially sent me this story in an E-mail. The Jerusalem Post subsequently published it on July 13, 2006.

THE SCULPTURE

Irma Shainberg Sheon

My husband and I never traveled to California without visiting his Uncle Bill and Aunt Sarah Sheon. When we arrived at their home in 1985, I was mesmerized by the picture of a contemporary male sculpture on the front of a catalogue that was lying on their coffee table. When I asked about it, Bob's aunt proudly said, "The model is my nephew, Howard Rosenberg."

A few days later, we arrived in Newport Beach at the home of cousins from my side of the family. My eyes widened when I spotted the very sculpture I had so recently admired. It was on a pedestal at the end of their entrance hall.

Twenty years later we attended a Sheon family reunion. During dinner in the hotel dining room, I heard Howard Rosenberg being introduced. I had never met him, but his features seemed familiar. I approached his table, waited for a break in the conversation, and timidly, half-covering my face, asked, "Did you ever sit for a sculptor?" Howard nearly jumped out of his seat and quickly responded, "Yes, once."

I proceeded to tell those at the table of my experience in the San Fernando Valley two decades ago. They did not know my story and had no knowledge of what had happened to the sculpture.

Suddenly Howard's ninety-year-old mother left the table and returned with the catalogue depicting the sculpture of her son. Everyone had been asked to bring memorabilia relating to the Sheon family to the reunion. She decided to bring the catalogue just for fun.

B'NAI ISRAEL
CONGREGATION

Harry Samuels

Often we are unable to appreciate examples of synchronicity while they're happening, but sometimes we are fortunate enough to be able to see the pieces of the puzzle fitting together into an overall design that affirms life's purpose.

While the far-reaching impact of connections between individuals is well documented, the impact of connections made by institutions can be far-reaching as well. One such example is that of a small synagogue in Cape Girardeau, Missouri: B'nai Israel Congregation. The positive effects that issued from that institution continue to impact people locally, nationally, and internationally.

Its story began in the 1930s when the synagogue was dedicated. At that time, approximately twelve Jewish families lived in the city of seventeen thousand, with an additional dozen in surrounding communities. With so few families, it was a hardship to maintain the congregation. The area's lack of such Jewish infrastructure as a community center, a Federation, or a youth organization made it difficult to maintain strong religious ties. B'nai Israel's prescient members recognized that these conditions could lead to rapid assimilation. To avert such an outcome, the congregation hired a young rabbi, but he left after a short time.

Lacking funds to engage another full-time rabbi, the congregation hired rabbis on an as-needed basis. One year Rabbi Leib Heber, who lived in Carbondale, Illinois, was asked to conduct the High Holy Day services. He had asked his rebbe, the late Rabbi Menachem Mendel Schneerson, if he should accept the invitation. The reply was clearly affirmative, and the answer he received he subsequently shared from the pulpit: "Remember that as children in Europe, we were given the task of placing lamps near overpasses and embankments. You should go to Cape Girardeau and light a candle because you never know whose path you might light up."

In the synagogue that day was an eleven year-old youth by the name of Alan Hecht. Rabbi Heber motivated Alan, who, along with other children in the congregation, began taking weekly Hebrew lessons from him. Years later, while studying at Hebrew University in Jerusalem, Alan called his parents: "There is no place to pray here," he told them. "Let's help establish a synagogue on Mount Scopus at Hebrew University."

The Martin Hecht family, his brother and sister-in-law, U.S. Senator & Mrs. Jacob "Chic" Hecht; and his sister and brother-in-law, Mr. & Mrs. Irvin Applebaum, made substantial financial commitments before seeking additional funding from the descendents of the founding families of the Cape synagogue.

In June 1981, the Hecht synagogue was dedicated and given to Hebrew University. One week later the synagogue witnessed its first *bar mitzvah*. (The ritual ceremony that marks the thirteenth birthday of a Jewish boy.) It was that of our son, David Samuels, of blessed memory, and it was the first bar mitzvah and first religious service conducted in the new facility.

In the foyer there is a plaque that reads, "In Honor of the Founders of the B'nai Israel Congregation, Cape Girardeau, Missouri, whose vision reached to Mt. Scopus." The founders listed include my parents, grandparents, and three sets of my aunts and uncles. Attending the dedication were Senator and Mrs. Jesse Helms from North Carolina who had been escorted by Martin and Chic Hecht and their wives.

As a Republican Senator, Chic saw much of Senator Helms whom many Jews considered to be a bigot and possibly anti-Semitic. Chic felt that Senator Helms didn't know many Jews since they represented such a small percentage of his constituency. That trip gave Senator and Mrs. Helms a better understanding of Israel. As an influential member of the Senate, he subsequently helped obtain significant support for Israel from the United States.

At that time, the Senate voted to sell A.W.A.C. airplanes—those with early warning devices—to Saudi Arabia. President Reagan asked Chic for his tie-breaking vote in support of the measure. Chic replied, "I will only do it if you assure me that it will not be detrimental to Israel." The president told him, "It will be not only not be harmful, it will be helpful." This was subsequently proven when those airplanes conveyed critical information to the U.S. and Israeli forces during operation Desert Storm." After the measure passed, President Regan told Chic, "You now hold my marker."

Chic decided that just as Jesse Helms hadn't understood Israel, neither did Premier Mikhail Gorbachev, the political leader of the Soviet Union, understand how badly the Jews of Russia wished to go to Israel. Chic proceeded to collect over twelve hundred names of Russian Jews wishing to emigrate. As President Reagan was about to leave for Iceland and a meeting with Premier Gorbachev,

Chic called in his marker. "Mr. President," he said, "here is a list of names I would like for you to personally give to the Premier. If you will do this for me, your marker will have been paid in full." Several weeks later, the first Jews were allowed to leave Russia.

In 2000, while on a Jewish Federation mission to Uzbekistan, I shared this story with Mr. Salai Meridor, Chairman of the Jewish Agency For Israel and recently the Israeli Ambassador to the United States. He said that he was well aware of these events but that "No one to my knowledge has publicly acknowledged Chic's contributions to the state of Israel."

Shortly after Chic's election to the Senate, he attended a farbrengen. *(Chassidic gathering.) Rabbi Schneerson predicted: "Senator you are going to accomplish important things for the Jewish people." Chic couldn't understand how this was to come about, but history has proven the Rebbe's words prophetic.*

The descendants of those founding members of the B'nai Israel Congregation have assumed leadership positions throughout the country and beyond. Martin Hecht continues to serve on the board of trustees of Hebrew University with the President of Israel.

With a lack of Jewish infrastructure, few peers, and no youth organizations, the normal assumption would have been for widespread and rapid assimilation; yet the opposite occurred. Of the twenty-six individuals whose lives I tracked, all married. There have been no inter-marriages, and no divorces.

While sitting beside the swimming pool of the King David Hotel in Jerusalem in 1981, Mr. Louis Hecht, Chic's father, shared the following story: "I came to Palestine and began taking pictures of synagogues. I wanted to build a synagogue in Cape Girardeau, and believed it would be helpful if we had some photographs to present to the architect. As I stood near the base of Mount Scopus, a lady asked, "What are you doing here?" I told her, "I am from Cape Girardeau, and I have a dream of someday building a synagogue in that small southeastern Missouri town." She responded, "I too, have a dream. I would like to someday build a hospital on top of this mountain." Her name was Henrietta Szold, the founder of Hadassah and its world famous Hadassah Hospital.

Since writing this story, we have learned of the death of Senator Chic Hecht. His legacy to Israel and the Jewish people continues to amortize.

THE TAPESTRY

Harry Samuels

While visiting the gift shop of the Jerusalem Hilton in 1981, my wife, Flora and I were attracted to a wall tapestry that depicted the skyline of the city. Flora observed, "Wouldn't that look good in our bedroom?"

After charging the purchase, I asked the salesman, "Could you roll it up so we can take it with us tomorrow on the plane?" "Sorry," the salesman replied, "the factory will have to mail it, but it will only take two weeks for delivery to your home."

A month later I wrote the factory, "Your salesman said we would receive our tapestry in two weeks. Please send it to us." There was no response.

Two months later, I asked a friend who is an attorney to send a letter on our behalf again requesting delivery. Again there was no response.

Three months later a friend of ours visited Jerusalem. When he asked about our purchase, the salesman in the gift shop told him, "We no longer carry that line. The factory will make it good."

In desperation I wrote the following letter to the factory:

"We were told by your sales representative at the Jerusalem Hilton that our tapestry would be received within two weeks of its purchase date. My subsequent letter to you, sent a month later, brought no response. The letter sent by my attorney two months after that, has been ignored. The personal request made by my friend three months later has never been acknowledged. If we do not receive the tapestry within the next three weeks, a curse will be placed upon you and your business."

It arrived in Memphis ten days later post-paid!

The tapestry had been charged on our Visa, and I understood that I could demand a refund, but we wanted it. My threat of a curse was not seriously intended. It was merely a device to get their attention. A few months later we learned that the firm had gone bankrupt.

THE ROLL

Murray Habbaz

The Arab woman living in Syria was distraught. Her drunkard husband would sit in the bathhouse until late each day before going home. One day he came home eating a roll.

"If you do not make me a cup of coffee before I finish eating this roll, I am going to divorce you," the man told his poor wife.

Terrified, she hurried to prepare the coffee, but her husband finished the roll before the coffee could be made. Enraged, the drunken husband shouted at her, "You are divorced from me," repeating it three times. This is the ancient formula for divorce prescribed by Islamic law. It forbids subsequent remarriage.

After the man became sober, he remembered what had happened and regretted his action. He went to the sheikh to ask if the divorce was valid, and was told that it was. "What can I do," he pleaded," Returning home he was so distraught, he took a different route than the one he usually traveled. On the way he met Rabbi Ezra Hamway, a very wise Jewish sage. "You look distressed," the rabbi said. "Perhaps I can be of help." After the man explained his problem, Rabbi Ezra agreed to offer his opinion—but only in the presence of the sheikh and the Moslem religious judge. When everyone was assembled, he asked the man," Was the roll you were eating fresh or dry?"

"It was dry."

"Then your wife is still married to you."

Everyone was amazed and wanted to know how Rabbi Ezra had come to such a conclusion.

The rabbi explained. "The man threatened to divorce his wife if she would not have the coffee ready by the time he finished eating the roll. But a dry roll makes crumbs. Since he did not eat the crumbs that fell on the floor, he never finished eating the roll. Therefore, the condition for his threat never came about, and the threat—that is, the divorce—does not apply."

My friend Murray Habbaz, the great-grandson of Rabbi Ezra, told me this story of an Arab benefiting from Talmudic thinking.

THE SPEEDER

Dr. Norman Shapiro

Dorothy Shapiro taught French at Southside High School in Memphis, Tennessee. She was a good teacher—amiable, but very strict. While on vacation and driving near Los Angeles, she heard a policeman's siren.

"Please pull over to the curb, and hand me your driver's license," he ordered.

"Officer," she pleaded with an exaggerated, slow, southern accent, "Can't you cut me a little slack and save those tickets for some of these city slickers?"

"Don't try to 'con' me Mrs. Shapiro," he replied. "I was your student at Southside."

ARTHUR AND CEIL

Harry Samuels

"I have found your book very interesting," said my newly discovered eighty-four year-old cousin, Arthur Sandberg. [*Beshert* that deals with true and remarkable stories]"You must know a lot of people."

He and his wife Ceil who had been married for sixty-five years were having lunch with us at Too J's, a popular delicatessen near Boca Raton, Florida.

"Arthur," I flippantly announced, "There must be at least two hundred people here today. Select anyone you wish, and I'll bet I can find a connection." It was a brash and spur-of-the-moment gesture, and the results surprised all of us."

"Don't I know you," he asked an elderly woman pushing a walker.

"I don't think so," she responded with an accent.

"Where are you from," I interjected.

"Berlin," she offered.

"Have you lived anywhere else," I questioned.

"Yes, I lived in Baltimore for thirty years."

I told her that during the Korean War a most hospitable family befriended me in Baltimore. I was stationed at Aberdeen Proving Grounds and spent many enjoyable weekends at their home. "Their name was Hoffberger," I offered. "Did you know anyone by that name?"

"Everyone knew the Hoffbergers of Baltimore," she chided. "Which ones did you know?"

"Charles C. Hoffberger," I answered.

It was apparent that she didn't believe me when she again questioned, "What was his wife's name?"

"Bernice," I responded.

"She was one of my closest friends," the lady gasped.

The Hoffberger family is recognized as one of the most outstanding in Baltimore. An uncle, Judge Joe Sherbow, played a significant role in registering a ship, the President Warfield, *in 1946, which was sent to France to take war survivors to Palestine. A* member of the Hoffberger family told me that the family helped supply the ship, whose name was later changed to The Exodus. It was subsequently made famous by the book and screenplay about the events in which it played a role. A monument in Baltimore's harbor area acknowledges its connection with the city.

Arthur and Ceil are charming. They are loaded with personality. Notwithstanding her severe affliction with Alzheimer's, they continue to play bridge. Arthur is completely devoted to his soul mate, and they share an apartment in an assisted living facility.

Following dinner in the dining room, Ceil walked to a piano and played several beautiful pieces using both her hands. "I have lived with her most of our lives," Arthur stated. "I never knew she could play the piano."

He is an avid fan of the Boston Red Sox. "You might want to know why people are not allowed to sit in the front rows of the bleachers at Fenway Park," he offered. "In 1972 the Red Sox were playing the Detroit Tigers. The teams were tied for first place, and that game decided the winner of the pennant. The score was tied when Reggie Smith hit a ball deep into center field where my daughter, Marilyn, and I were sitting in the first row. The ball headed toward Marilyn when a man next to her held up his hand to protect her. The ball bounced into the playing field, and Reggie's home run was ruled a ground rule triple. He failed to score, and the Tigers won the pennant by one-half a game.

THE POST CARD

Leonid and Friderica Saharovici

Leonid and Friderica Saharovici lived in Bucharest, Romania. In 1970 while visiting several relatives in Memphis, dinner parties were held in their honor. In January 1972, they moved to Memphis permanently and established reputations as two of its outstanding citizens.

They often attend estate sales seeking old books, manuscripts, and documents that help define a previous era. In 2003 they noticed an advertisement in the classified section of the newspaper announcing an estate sale. The address was not familiar, and the name of the previous owner was unfamiliar.

As they walked through the house, Leonid's eyes were suddenly riveted by a picture post card wedged under the frame of a mirror. "It is a picture of a street scene in Bucharest that was only one block from our old house," he exclaimed.

"I don't believe this," Friderica gasped. "Look at the signature! I sent this card to Mrs. Abe Alperin thirty-three years ago—thanking her for her hospitality to us when we first came here."

PART V
FAITH

SERENDIPITY
AND THE REBBE

Rabbi Marc Wilson

The following story recounts an experience of Rabbi Marc Howard Wilson, a rabbi and syndicated columnist in Greenville, South Carolina, who granted permission for its use. His essays can be found at MarcMusing.com.

"I make no apologies for my devotion to Chasidism, particularly to the Chabad-Lubavitch movement because of its tireless outreach and nonjudgmental welcome to all Jews. Moreover, it asks nothing in return."

"Do I agree with every point of the movement's theology and lifestyle? No, but enough to make me an adherent. In fact, you could call me a 'closet Lubavitcher.'

All Lubavitchers consider the movement's most recent Rebbe, the late Menachem Schneerson, as irreplaceable. Do they consider him a miracle worker or perhaps a great cosmic influence? Is he the messiah? This is a subject of tremendous controversy, even condemnation, in the secular media and other Jewish movements. Let's simply say that many Lubavitchers openly declare him the messiah, while for others the idea hovers as a distinct possibility.

"Two years before his death, the Rebbe became my 'savior.' In a scant thirty seconds, he stroked my arm and offered me guidance at the most dismal time of my life. Those few words, I now realize, marked the beginning of my emotional and spiritual restoration.

"A few months ago, I spent a week in New York working on a project. My driver to the airport was a young Lubavitcher. At the sight of my yarmulke, he asked whether I had ever visited the *ohel* (the Rebbe's tomb.) I told him I had not, but if we had time, I would like to pay my respects. Knowing that people flock there to ask for the Rebbe's intercession, and remembering his lifesaving advice for me, it was the least I could do.

At the tomb, my driver recommended that I write a request to be placed on the Rebbe's tomb. So I prayed for universal peace and for the safety of my family.

Then I asked for something out of the ordinary: Three years earlier, I had departed from my congregation in Greenville under acrimonious, even crazy, circumstances. Many congregants were angry. Some had forgiven me, and our relationships had slowly resumed. For others, the anger still burned. But the Goldberg's[1] with whom my wife and I were particularly close and whose friendship we cherished, stopped talking to us and refused all pleas of forgiveness.

"So I prayed that there would be reconciliation with the congregants who were still estranged and particularly for forgiveness from the Goldbergs. I dropped the shredded request, as is the custom, on the tomb and noted that it was 6 p.m., time to leave for the airport. Shortly thereafter, I called Linda to tell her that the plane was departing on time.

'You'll never guess who called,' she announced. 'The Goldbergs.'

"Astonished, I asked her if there had been any particular reason."

'No. It was an incredible surprise. They just wanted to say hello.'

"And do you remember about what time they called?"

'It must have been around 6:05.'

"My personal feelings aside, relating this wonder story is not meant to persuade anyone to believe in miracles, nor to believe that the Rebbe is the messiah or that I was at all worthy of divine intercession. I have only one purpose: It is to tell people who are smug or doubting that we never know. We expect, and we never know. Life wearies us, and we never know."

I just spoke with Toni Gruner whose husband, Larry was in desperate need of a quadruple bi-pass when it was discovered that his kidneys were about to shut down. The heart surgeons could not proceed until the kidneys were functioning. Tony began looking for a living donor among the children. She called Rabbi Levi Klein who was attending a conference in New Jersey. Prior to receiving her call, Rabbi Klein had decided to stay in New York another day to visit his parents. After speaking with Toni, he said," I will go to the Rebbe's gravesite and say prayers on behalf of your husband," Early the following morning, the nephrologist entered Larry's hospital room. Grinning, he said, "A miracle has occurred. Your husband's kidneys are functioning again. Now we can proceed with the heart surgery." When Rabbi Klein was told the good news he remarked, "Now I know why I stayed in New York another day."
I am personally aware of four others who have recently had similar experiences. An eleven-year-old girl in Maryland with a brain tumor who is currently a star soccer player; my nephew in St. Louis with pancreatic cancer who is playing golf and tennis

---

1.   Pseudonym

again; a seven year-old boy in Florida with AML (leukemia) who has been pro-nounced free of cancer; and my wife who suffered from a brain tumor and is now beating me in tennis.

Skeptics will attribute the recovery of these patients—following the intervention of Rabbi Klein—to the placebo effect in addition to the conventional therapies they received. I have no answers; only questions.

THE PACKAGE

Rabbi Manis Friedman

Rabbi Manis Friedman told this story at a religious retreat last year. The rabbi in the story was the father of Rabbi Friedman's teacher.

"Many years ago, the atheistic government of Russia banned religious practices. One day, a pious Jew was caught building a *Mikvah* (ritual bath) and was exiled to live in the Arctic for twelve years.

During that arduous period, he was determined to observe his religious practices. The Arctic natives, who saw him, called him a holy man. They invited him to live in their shelter, curtaining off a space for him with a reindeer skin. On Friday nights, they gave him a kerosene lamp to light, symbolic of the Sabbath candles that are traditionally lit at that time.

Soon *Pesach* (Passover) was approaching. In years past, the rabbi's wife sent him *matzos* (unleavened bread) to eat, but this year the *matzos* didn't come.

The natives knew his food consisted only of bread and without the *matzo* substitute, they feared the Rabbi might starve. Each day they checked for the missing package.

The day before *Pesach*, a message came to the government headquarters that an official was arriving that day by ship. Someone was needed to drive a sled to the dock and pick him up. As it was the beginning of spring, the ice was melting and it was dangerous to drive a heavy load. The driver was instructed NOT to bring any packages from the post office.

As the driver was ready to return with his passenger, the postman stopped him and said, 'you must take this package with you. It is the most important-looking package I have ever seen. Look at all the official stamps on it. If you don't take it, we might all be in trouble.' Reluctantly, the driver took the box and delivered it to his outpost. It was the Rabbi's *matzos*.

The reason for the mysterious stamps was this: The Russian officials who mailed the package didn't want it to arrive on time. Anticipating this, the rabbi's wife mailed it several months in advance. Instead of sending the package north, the quickest route, it was intentionally misdirected to the south by the authorities. At every postal stop, the package was stamped. By the time it reached the Arctic, it was completely covered and most impressive looking."

THE MOHEL

RabbI Yosef Kantor

One day, while serving in Bangkok, Rabbi Yosef C. Kantor was riding in a taxi that had become stuck in heavy traffic. Calculating that it would take less time to walk to his destination, he paid the fare and got out. As he was walking down the street, a well-dressed foreigner approached him.

"Excuse me for stopping you on the street like this," the man began. "It is just that you look like you could help me. My wife and I are from America, and we have a business here. We are expecting the birth of a baby boy any day now. Where would we be able to find a *mohel*?" (One qualified to perform male circumcisions in accordance with Jewish law).

"I am a *mohel*," the rabbi replied with a smile, "and I will be happy to be of service."

The man told the rabbi of his wife's conversation of the previous day. She had anxiously questioned her husband, "Have you done anything more to find a *mohel*? What do you expect? Do you think you will bump into one on the streets of Bangkok?"

THE PRIEST

Chana Weisberg

"Almost thirty years ago," writes Chana Weisberg, "my father, Rabbi Dovid Schochet was asked to deliver a lecture to a group including both Jews and non-Jews in Buffalo. Because of its universal application to both Jews and gentiles, he decided to focus his lecture on the theme of charity. My father began with the following story:

"A wealthy individual from Prague who never contributed to charity lived during the time of the Tosfos Yom Tov, a great Jewish sage. After the miser died, the *Chevra Kaddisha* (the society responsible for the burial) felt that he was unworthy of being interred next to any upright and respectable individual. They buried him, instead, in the area of the cemetery called *hekdesh,* reserved for society's outcasts.

A few days after the funeral, a tumult developed in the city. The butcher and baker, two prominent members of the community, who had hitherto been extremely charitable, suddenly stopped distributing their funds. The poor people, who had relied on the benevolent pair for their sustenance, now were in a state of uproar. Emotions ran so deep that the matter was finally brought before the Tosfos Yom Tov.

He asked the two men why they had so abruptly terminated their benevolent acts." They replied: "In the past, this 'miser' would continuously supply us with funds for charity. He strongly warned us, however, not to disclose our source since he wanted the great merit of performing the *mitzvah* (commandment or good deed) in a hidden manner. Now that he is dead, unfortunately, we are no longer able to continue."

"Awed by the unassuming 'miser's' behavior, the Tosfos Yom Tov requested that he be buried next to this humble man, even though this meant being interred in an undesirable section of the cemetery."

As my father concluded his lecture, a participant from the audience, who happened to be a priest, approached him and requested that he repeat the story. My father suggested they meet the following day. Thinking that the matter would be forgotten, my father was surprised when, at the appointed hour, the priest arrived at the hotel.

The priest, once again, pleaded with my father to repeat the story. My father obliged, but was astounded when, after concluding the story a second time, the priest seemed terribly distraught and begged him to repeat it, yet again.

At this point, the priest was nervously pacing back and forth across the room. Finally, he divulged the reason for his agitation. He turned to my father and confessed, "Rabbi Schochet, that charitable man in the story was my ancestor."

Skeptically, my father calmed the young man assuring him that there was absolutely no connection between him and the story, which took place over a hundred years ago.

"Furthermore," he told him, "you're a gentile, while this man was Jewish."

The priest looked intently at my father and whispered, "Rabbi, now I have a story to tell you."

He began by describing his background. He had grown up in Tennessee. His father was a major in the U.S. army during World War ll. Overseas, in Europe, his father, a Catholic, had met a Jewish girl and had fallen in love. He brought her back home as his war bride, and no one knew of her background. A short time after their marriage, the couple was blessed with a child, whom they raised devoutly in the Catholic tradition. The child grew up and attended a seminary where he eventually became a priest.

In his early adulthood, the priest's mother died. On her deathbed, she disclosed her secret identity to her completely baffled son: "I want you to know that you are Jewish."

She informed him of his heritage and that his great-grandfather was buried next to a great sage called the Tosfos Yom Tov. She then recounted, almost verbatim, the story that my father had told in his lecture. At the time, the priest imagined that his mother was delirious. Although he was disturbed by his mother's parting words, he felt the need to get on with his life and put the story behind him.

"Rabbi," cried the priest, in a state of complete emotional upheaval, "you have just repeated this story, detail for detail, you have reminded me of my mother's parting words, and that the story must be true. Yet what am I to do? I am a reputable priest with a large congregation of devoted followers."

My father offered to assist him in any way he could. He emphasized to him, however, that according to Judaism, he was indeed Jewish. He encouraged him to explore his heritage, and put him in contact with people in his city who could guide him. With that, the weary, newly found Jew departed. My father had no further correspondence with this man, and heard no more from him.

Several years ago, on a visit to Israel, a bearded, religious Jew approached my father at the Western Wall, and wished him, "*Shalom Alechem,*" (peace be with you.) My father didn't recognize the individual and was completely taken aback when the man exclaimed, "Don't you recognize me, Rabbi Schochet? I'm the former priest whom you met in Buffalo!"

Chana Weisberg generously allowed me to excerpt this story from her new book, Divine Whispers—Stories That Speak to the Heart and Soul.

LECHA DODI

Zev Roth

This story is taken from the book, *Monsey, Kiryat Sefer and Beyond*, by Zev Roth, who kindly allowed me to present it here.

Lecha Dodi is the title of a mystical poem written in 1571. It is set to song in which the Sabbath is personified as a bride who visits the faithful of Israel. She is honored and made welcome. The Hebrew words of the first sentence translate: "Come, my friend, to meet the bride; let us welcome the presence of the Sabbath." It is sung every Friday night throughout the Jewish world. During the rendition of the last stanza, the singer stands and faces the rear in a welcoming gesture. (Prayers are recited while facing toward the site of the Holy Temple in Jerusalem.) As Rabbi Lewis Kraut[1] faced the rear of the Israeli synagogue that Friday night, he noticed a young man who seemed lonely and somewhat nervous. He was dressed in jeans and was carrying a backpack. With a dark complexion and thick unruly black hair, he appeared to have been of Portuguese or Spanish origin.

Rabbi Kraut had learned not to ask too many questions of young people. He merely extended his hand and said, "My name is Lewis Kraut and I would like to invite you to our home for a traditional *Shabbat* (Sabbath) meal. How does that grab you?"

"It sounds good to me," the youth replied, gathering his few possessions and walking beside his host.

As they stood beside the dinner table with the rest of the family singing traditional songs, the rabbi noticed that his guest was not joining in the singing. "Maybe he's shy or just can't sing," he surmised.

When they went into the kitchen to "wash" (a ritual of pouring water over the hands prior to reciting a blessing.) The boy seemed to be unfamiliar with the custom.

During the meal, he seemed uneasy and was mainly silent.

---

1. Pseudonym

"Is there a melody you would like to sing?" Rabbi Kraut asked.

"There is a song I really like. It was sung this evening in the synagogue. It was called like *Dodi* something."

The rabbi paused for a moment, on the verge of saying, "It's not usually sung at the table," but then he caught himself. "If that's what the kid wants," he thought, "what's the harm?" Aloud he said, "You mean *Lecha Dodi*. Wait, let me get you a prayer book."

After singing *Lecha Dodi* the young man remained silent until after the soup course when he was again asked if he had another favorite melody.

"Could we sing *Lecha Dodi* again there is something about that song that intrigues me." For the remainder of the meal, they must have sung *Lecha Dodi* seven or eight times.

Just as the rabbi thought, the young man didn't have a place to sleep that night. He invited him to stay at his home. During the meal the next day, the guest continued to request the singing of *Lecha Dodi*. After Sabbath concluded, Rabbi Kraut asked, "Where are you from?" The young man looked pained. He stared down at the floor and softly said, "Ramallah."

He thought he heard his guest say "Ramallah." an Arab city. "He must have said 'Ramleh,' an Israeli city," he imagined. "I have a cousin there. Do you know Ephriam Warner?" The guest shook his head sadly. "There are no Jews in Ramallah!"

"I must be confused," he told the boy." I haven't asked your name." He answered quietly, "Machmud Ibn-esh-Sharif. "Lewis didn't know what to do. "Should I call the police? Throw him out of my house? What is that in his backpack? Is he a terrorist?"

Machmud began to speak. "Would you like to hear my story? I was born and grew up in Ramallah. I was taught to hate my Jewish oppressors, and to believe that killing them was an act of heroism. But I always had my doubts. I mean, we were taught that the Sunni tradition says, 'No one of you is a believer until he desires for his brother that which he desires for himself.' I used to sit and wonder, weren't the Jews people too? Didn't they have the right to live the same as we? If we're supposed to be good to everyone, how come nobody includes Jews in that? I was in class one day when I raised one of these questions. The Imam had a simple answer. In front of everybody, he slapped me so hard I nearly passed out. Eventually they threw me out of the school, and my father threw me out of the house.

"I decided to run away and live with the Jews so I could learn more about them and their religion. When I sneaked back home to pack, my mother caught me. I told her of my plan. I said that I might even decide to convert."

"You don't have to convert," she told me. "You are already Jewish."

I couldn't understand. "What do you mean?" I asked.

She told me that she had been born Jewish and had married an Arab. "According to Jewish law," she said, "a child born of a Jewish mother is Jewish, therefore you, too, are a Jew." She dug out some old documents and handed them to me; things like my birth certificate and her old Israeli ID card, so I could prove I was a Jew. I've got them here, but I don't know what to do with them."

"Also," he added, "my mother hesitated over one piece of paper. Handing it to me she said, 'Take this too. It's an old photograph of my grandparents. I was told it was made when they went looking for the grave of some great ancestor of ours in the north.'"

Rabbi Kraut gently put his hand on Machmud's shoulder. Machmud looked up, scared and hopeful at the same time. The Lewis asked," Do you have the photo here?"

The boys face lit up." Sure! I always carry it with me." Reaching into his backpack he pulled out an old, tattered envelope.

The rabbi adjusted his glasses and examined the photograph. Centered in the picture was a Sephardic family from the turn of the century. They were standing around a grave in the old cemetery of Safed. As he focused on the gravestone inscription, Rabbi Kraut's heart beat excitedly. Looking up at Machmud he explained, "This is the grave of Rabbi Shlomoh Alkabetz, a great sage and your ancestor, who was the author of *Lecha Dodi!*"

I asked Rabbi Lazar Shore, of blessed memory, if there were any other reasons for the tradition of facing the rear of the synagogue while reciting the last stanza of Lecha Dodi. *He replied with the answer his rebbe had given him in Europe, "Years ago, the more affluent members of congregations sat near the front of the synagogues. When they turned around, they were able to see those in the assembly who appeared to be in need of companionship or a good meal."*

THE WEEKEND

Rabbi Levi Klein

"I'm calling from the Memphis airport," said the voice on the telephone late Friday afternoon. "Our plane has been delayed, and it is impossible to return home before the start of the Sabbath. Do you have accommodations for us at your home?"

Rabbi Levi Klein replied, "Of course you can stay with us. I will pick you up at the airport."

"Incidentally," the stranger added, "there is a young lady traveling with me."

"We have room for her, too," the rabbi added. Since the weekend led to a two-day holiday, the visit was extended.

A year later, the Kleins received a thank you note. It read as follows:

"When you extended yourselves to us last year, Maurice and I were returning from a trip to the islands. We had been dating for a long time and had planned to end our relationship. But since we had already paid for the vacation, we decided to make the trip. We enjoyed your hospitality and meeting your beautiful family. We decided that we, too, wished to have such a family and to establish a Jewish home such as yours. We have since married and are expecting our first child. Thank you."

Rabbi Levi Klein is the spiritual leader of the Chabad Lubavitch Congregation of Memphis, Tennessee. He is one of the most caring and dynamic individuals I have ever met.

RELIGIOUS OBJECTS

Edward Lindberg

It is July 3, 2006, and my mail includes a letter sent by a stranger from another city. "I have just finished reading *Beshert*," he said, "and would like to share my story with you. Feel free to use it if you write another book:

One of my middle-aged friends is a wholesaler of antiques. He is not Jewish, but felt it would be wrong to sell a box of Jewish religious items he had obtained as part of an estate sale. The box contained a huge black and white tallis (prayer shawl), the type I had always admired when seeing them enveloping pious old men. Additionally, there was a pair of large, old t'fillin (phylacteries). Both items looked as if they had been waiting for someone who never returned to claim them. He insisted I take them, and I put them into the trunk of my car.

On a late Friday afternoon in August I left Atlanta, where I had been working, and headed to my home in Chattanooga. I placed my briefcase and bag of laundry in the trunk, and for some unknown reason I put the box with the religious items on the passenger seat next to me. The traffic on I-75 was murderous.

Within an hour I was involved in a potentially catastrophic automobile accident. As I passed a truck at high speed, with all lanes of the freeway filled side to side and with bumper-to-bumper traffic, I heard a great crashing noise. Glass was in the air around me, and I thought there had been an explosion. I subsequently learned that a short length of steel I-beam had sailed through my windshield striking me slightly, but totally blinding me in the explosion of shattered glass from my windshield. There was no rational explanation for a terrified and blinded man to be able to safely maneuver his fast moving car leftward across lanes of speeding traffic, but I did.

I called 911 on my cell phone and was assured that help was on its way. When the firemen and police arrived, they washed my face and eyes. They seemed surprised I was not dead or mortally injured. One officer looked at the length of steel lying on the back floor of my car and said, 'Mister, every man here will tell you there's no reason for you to be alive. You should have been killed. G-d must love you.'

85

It was then I noticed the open box, the *tallis* and *t'fillin*, sitting on the seat undisturbed beneath a pile of glass shards that glistened like spilled diamonds. I knew at that moment that I was going to be all right. I knew also that I was very blessed.

I covered the remaining glass windshield with shipping tape and proceeded north. I recited a prayer of thanksgiving for my deliverance from death and touched the holy object several times."

Jewish tradition affirms that keeping a holy book or religious objects in a car lends protection.

PART VI
WAR

THE HOLOCAUST

Leonid and Friderica Saharovici

In April 1993, Leonid and Friderica Saharovici visited the Yad Vashem Memorial to the Holocaust in Jerusalem. A good friend, Dr. Lustig, guided them through the portion of the museum dedicated to the 1,500,000 children who were slaughtered. He told them of the tragic fate of Eva Heyman, a young girl born in 1931 whose diary closely resembles that of the celebrated Anne Frank. Her story was published in a book, *I Lived So Little*. Oliver Lustig, brother of their guide, translated it into Romanian. The Saharovicis were deeply moved by the experience, and as they wept, Mr. Lustig handed them a copy of Eva's book. Since they are both from Romania, it was especially meaningful to them, and they treasured it.

The following month they participated in the dedication of the U.S. Holocaust Museum in Washington, D.C. As they began a five-hour tour of that magnificent memorial, each of them was issued a victim's identification card. The cards are drawn from a dispensing machine and contain the names and details of a Holocaust victim the same age as the visitor. Its purpose is to enable each visitor to identify more closely with a particular victim, thereby making the visit more meaningful and memorable. Imprinted on the back of each card is the following: "This card tells the story of a real person who lived during the Holocaust. Please carry it with you and update the story at each of the three printing stations located on the fourth and second floors of the exhibition." At the end of the visit, the last machine to update the information explains the final destiny of that individual.

"I don't believe this," Friderica sobbed. "Look." Imprinted on card number 4141 that she received that day was the name, Eva Heyman.

Prompted by this experience, Leonid recalled the quote, "One death is a tragedy; one million deaths is a statistic." He and his wife are survivors of the Holocaust. He represented the state of Tennessee at the opening of the U.S. Holocaust Museum, and is the founder of the Tennessee Commission for Holocaust Education

TAMAR

Flora Samuels

We met Professor Aryeh Kasher and his wife, Tamar in 1991 at Memphis State University. We were serving dinner to a group of students at the Jewish Student Union building. The Kashers had just arrived from Israel where Dr. Kasher served as professor of history at Tel Aviv University. He had come to Memphis as a visiting scholar with the local Judaic studies program.

After dinner, we invited the Kashers to our home to become better acquainted. As we began exchanging *beshert* stories, Tamar said, "I had a strange experience recently. Prior to coming to Memphis, we lived in Columbus, Ohio. While waiting in my dentist's office there, I began looking at some old magazines piled on a table. One publication was missing its cover, but it was filled with interesting black and white photographs. When I opened it to the centerfold, my heart began pounding and tears came to my eyes. The picture, taken in 1948, showed several people in Jerusalem amidst wreckage caused by an explosion. Prominently shown in the photograph was a picture of my father rescuing a child."

"Just a minute," interrupted my wife, Flora, hurrying from the room. She quickly returned holding an old copy of *Life Magazine* containing the photograph of Tamar's father. The fact that Tamar was unaware of the name of the publication and that Flora had saved the magazine—never having seen a photo of Tamar's father, added to that unexpected and exciting moment.

BOMBS AWAY

Wikipedia Encyclopedia

While walking early one morning, I listened to a radio program describing an incident that occurred during the early years of World War ll.

Hitler was determined to destroy the Royal Air Force by obliterating its infrastructure of airfields and factories. He understood that without air power for protection, England would be much easier to conquer. The constant air raids were helping him achieve his objectives. The R.A.F. was stretched thin and would soon have become ineffective had not a German bomber pilot inadvertently dropped some bombs on the outskirts of London. The pilot was running low on fuel and thought he was lightening his load in an undeveloped area—not London.

England retaliated immediately by bombing Berlin. Hitler then became so incensed; he diverted his entire air power away from the R.A.F. infrastructure and toward the destruction of London. This gave the British air force the time needed to recover.

Do you believe the pilot of that airplane realized the significant role he played in Germany's ultimate defeat?

THOU SHALT NOT COVET

Sharon Tabachnick

Sharon Tabachnick acknowledges that she is alive today because her grandfather had been too poor to build a house in the Jewish area of Bucharest, Romania.

"I really would like to build a home for myself and one for my son and his family," he declared, "but I can't afford the cost of the land near the Jewish homes of our city. Perhaps if I build in the poorer part of town my new neighbors will accept us."

He did build a home for his family, and one for his son's family. They developed good relationships in their new location.

The fascist militia, the Iron Guard, which was allied with the Nazis, came to destroy the Jews of the city. They failed to look for Jews in the "less desirable" area. None of the neighbors of Sharon's family alerted the authorities.

THE RIGHTEOUS ONE

Harry Samuels

Prior to attending the wedding of our cousin in Bethesda, Maryland, we toured the newly opened National Holocaust Museum. As we neared the end of the tour, we noticed a semi-partition studded with numerous small plaques. Each one described an act of heroism performed during the Holocaust by a non-Jew—a righteous gentile—whose act of heroism was commemorated. There was time to read only a few stories, but one caught our eye. It told of Irene Opdyke, a lady from Tarnopol, Poland, who saved thirteen Jews whom she had hidden in the basement of her home.

A Nazi major came to see her one-day. "I know what you're doing," he informed her. "If you will agree to become my mistress, I won't tell the authorities." She agreed, and all of the thirteen people were saved.

We rushed from the museum to attend the wedding festivities. The following evening, during the rehearsal dinner, we overheard someone telling her mother that her cousin was still living in New York City.

"You know," she continued, "she was one of thirteen people saved by a non-Jewish lady in Poland whose home was occupied by a Nazi Major. She kept them in her basement and protected them by extending sexual favors to that officer."

WITH THE GRENADIERS

Sir Winston Churchill

During the First World War, Winston Churchill served with the Grenadier Guards as a major. He was stationed in France near the front lines when he received an order to meet with the Corp Commander. Though he could not imagine the reason for the order since he had joined his unit only four days earlier. Nevertheless he proceeded to trudge three miles across muddy fields to the place where the General's car was to meet him. After waiting an hour in the rain and sleet, a Staff Officer approached.

"Are you Major Churchill?" he asked.

"Yes," he replied.

"There was a mistake," he said. "Your car went to the wrong place. You can return to your unit."

"Would you please tell me why the General wanted me out of the line?" Churchill chided.

"It was nothing in particular," the officer responded. "He only wanted a chat, and said another day would do equally well."

Churchill was quite indignant until he learned that soon after leaving for the meeting, a shell had exploded only a few feet from where he would have been sitting.

"Suddenly my irritation toward the General passed completely. and then upon these quaint reflections there came the strong sensation that a hand had been stretched out to move me in the nick of time from a fatal spot. But whether it was the General's hand or not, I cannot tell."

This incident saved the life of Winston Churchill whose leadership during World War II greatly impacted the future of England and Western civilization

Prior to volunteering for the army, Churchill served as a highly regarded war correspondent, Member of Parliament, Home Secretary, and First Lord of the Admiralty. In view of these credentials, it is not surprising that the Corp Commander wished to meet with him.

This story occurred in 1915 and was published in Great Destiny by G.P. Putnam's Son. Curtiss Brown Ltd., UK literary agents for the Estate of Sir Winston Churchill, kindly permitted its inclusion.

PART VII
A MIX

THE ZIPPER

Bob Rosenthal

As a young teenager during the mid 40s, Bob worked after school in the men's store operated by his father and uncle. At that time, zippers were replacing buttons on men's trousers. Stories abounded of painful incidents occurring when this new fangled device was employed, and many men refused to subject themselves to the danger.

To convince customers they were safe, Bob's uncle devised a clever though unorthodox plan. He purchased a rabbit's foot and sewed it on the front of his nephew's under shorts. To demonstrate the safety of the zipper to a prospective purchaser, Bob was instructed to come to the dressing room where he would unzip, show the rabbit's foot, and zip up "safely."

A customer selected a pair of Botany trousers, their most expensive, but he insisted on a button fly. "I have heard of men being hurt badly by this thing," he said, "It isn't going to happen to me!"

"But sir," the owners implored, "Zippers are perfectly safe, and besides they're warmer. We've heard stupid stories of men being hurt by zippers, but nothing like that ever happened. Isn't that right Bobby?"

"Right," Bob said. "They're perfectly safe, and besides they're warmer in cold weather."

"Show this gentleman how it works," his uncle commanded.

Bob climbed onto a footstool, unzipped his pants and pulled out the rabbit's foot. When he proceeded to zip up, the hairs of the device were caught tearing an inch off the rabbit's foot.

The customer's eyes bulged and he kept repeating, "Oh my G-d, Oh my G-d ..." over and over. "I'm never going to buy any of these pants. I'll believe that zippers are safe when somebody can fly to the moon and walk on it!"

His uncle was furious. Bob tried to calm him by pointing out that in the serial currently playing at the Lincoln Theater; Flash Gordon had gone to the moon.

"No one has ever gone to the moon," his uncle roared, "Nor would anyone ever go to the moon."

At that moment Bob became determined someday to help send a man to the moon, and he did!

Bob Rosenthal became an engineer and ultimately a key member of the Apollo development team. He has had a fascinating career as an aircraft designer, a rocket scientist, a spacecraft developer and a high-tech entrepreneur. He is an award-winning humorist for his books, short stories and lectures. When I asked his permission to use this anecdote, he was most cordial and agreeable. It was taken from his book, From Passaic to the Moon: An Insider's True Adventures.

THE MORTGAGE

Harry Samuels

My friend Al operated a children's shop in St. Louis. I had come to buy some fill-ins for our store in Jonesboro, Arkansas. "How's your business?" I asked. "It's terrible," he replied. "There's a large membership department store that's underselling me. You can borrow my membership card if you'd like to see it."

Four hours later, I had made a study of the operation and was extremely impressed. I had drawn a floor plan of the place and had learned the names of most of the lessees. On a subsequent visit to Memphis, I explained the operation to my cousin, Howard Waller, and urged him and his associates to build a replica in Memphis.

"I'll build it if you manage it," he offered. Six months later we opened the Dixiemart Store in Memphis. It was the largest membership department store in the United States at that time. The store flourished. After a couple of months of operation, Howard said, "In addition to your salary, I'm going to pay you one percent of the net profit for the first year. This is to reimburse you for your efforts in helping us to establish the business." I never expected to receive anything from that gesture since initial expenses incurred in a new business normally wipe out net profit.

Five years later, my wife and I contracted to purchase a larger home for our growing family. We needed a mortgage in order to buy the $45,000.00 property.

"How much will you lend us?" I asked the banker.

"I can give you a 75% mortgage at a 5% rate with a 20 year loan term," he replied, "but you'll be required to pay down $11,250.00."

I had planned to borrow the entire down payment, but prior to contacting my friends and family for the money, I called the comptroller of Dixiemart. "Did I earn anything from that one percent net profit I was promised?" I inquired." I'm sure I was never paid any part of it."

"Let me check our books, and I'll let you know," he replied. A few minutes later he told me, "You earned exactly $ 11,250.00!"

WRONG NUMBER

Jeff Baum

Jeff Baum made a professional visit to the office of a physician in Memphis. As he waited to be seen, the telephone rang.

"It's for you Jeff," the secretary said.

"How could anyone know to reach me here," he pondered. "I didn't know I was coming here myself until a few minutes ago."

The caller said, "I was calling you to place an order, and I was given this number."

Jeff's number was 795-6100; the customer dialed 795-5100 by mistake.

LIFE SAVERS

Sidney Kriger

The retinal surgeon, Dr. Richard Sievers, scooted back his stool after examining a patient. At that moment, his white lab coat caught under one of the stool's wheels causing him to be thrown backward against the sharp edge of a desk.

"Ouch! That really hurt," he exclaimed. "I hope it didn't do any permanent damage."

For several weeks he waited for the pain to subside. Finally, he visited Dr. Lynn Conrad, a urologist and friend, to determine if he had seriously injured his kidney.

"The ultrasound doesn't indicate any serious damage to your left side, but since you're here, let's check the other side," Dr. Conrad suggested.

"You're a lucky guy Dick," he said. "I believe I detect a tumor on your other kidney! You might not have found it had you not fallen."

Dr. Sievers shared with me another life-saving experience that involved his friend, Dr. Conrad. The latter had attended a national convention with a large number of urologists. From the front of the room a request was made for someone to allow himself to be tested on a new portable ultrasound machine that was being presented. No one responded until Dr. Conrad reluctantly agreed to be tested. When the image of his kidneys was displayed on the large screen, the group was amazed to see before them the indication of a tumor that had not previously been detected.
Both of these men are practicing medicine and doing well. They were extremely cordial when I requested permission to cite their stories.

THE SONG

Ted Roberts

"I remember going to a movie with my father in 1937," Ted Roberts told me. "The theme song of the show was *The First Time I Met You*. My father would hum and sing excerpts from that song at every opportunity for the remainder of his life. That melody haunted me long after my father's death. I would ask bandleaders to play that tune, but no one was familiar with it or knew where it had originated."

"One evening last year, I distinctly remember turning off the television and the downstairs lights before climbing up the stairs to our bedroom. At 1:00 a.m., I awoke to loud noises. I thought there were intruders and cautiously descended the stairs to investigate. As I slowly crept into the den, I realized that the noise was coming from the television set. It was playing a movie, *The Toast of New York*. The song that was being played was *The First Time I Met You!*"

Ted Roberts is a friend and syndicated Jewish columnist from Huntsville, Alabama. His Thoughts of Ted Roberts *appear in seventy-four national, regional and Jewish publications as well as on National Public Radio. For a treat, I urge you to access his blog site: (scribblerontheroof.typepad.com). He is a worthy successor to the late Harry Golden.*

THE INVENTORY

Harry Samuels

My business partner and best friend, Vic Shainberg, and I began to operate stores in Jonesboro, Arkansas, in 1956. In 1961, we hired managers for our stores while we proceeded to help develop and manage the first major membership department stores in Memphis. We had been very happy in Jonesboro, and our plans were ultimately to return to our businesses.

One day I received a frantic call from Vic, "We have a problem in Jonesboro. I just received the inventory figures for the department store, and it's short ten thousand dollars. What are we going to do about it?" At that time we felt that such a shortage could only have been generated internally. It was apparent that we either had to return to Jonesboro, take over management, or sell our stores.

We immediately began the process of selling, and a few weeks later we held a very successful going out of business sale. We contracted to sell the remaining stock and fixtures, and began taking inventory to determine the value of the merchandise.

After checking and recording the inventory for several hours, Vic rushed over with a big smile. "We just found the missing items," he proudly exclaimed. "Someone forgot to take the shoe inventory on the balcony!"

Initially we were upset—having felt compelled to sell our interests in Jonesboro. We had enjoyed the city with our many friends and thought we might wish to return to our businesses there someday.

Subsequently we considered it a blessing, as we spent the remainder of our lives in Memphis. There, we married, reared our children, and became happily involved in the community.

THE ROSE

Aviva Garfine

A few years ago I was at a crossroads in my life. One road was particularly challenging with many attendant doubts and fears. One Sunday I visited a good friend whose opinion I valued. After a lengthy conversation, she urged me to follow the more difficult road. When I hesitated she said, "You must have faith in the universe. Believe in yourself and your guardian angels will give you a sign." "What kind of sign will it be?" I asked skeptically. "I'm not sure—maybe a flower," she added.

"I always drive with my windows down. As I stopped for a traffic light, a man selling flowers approached with a bouquet and asked, "Lady, would you like to buy some flowers?" I responded, "No, thank you," whereupon he presented me with a rose saying, "This is for you." Momentarily stunned by his gesture I asked him, "Why did you hand me this rose?" "I really don't know," he replied.

"The traffic light changed, and before I could say more, the cars honking behind me forced me to speed away.

At that moment my decision became clear. This was the sign from my guardian angel—who was I to argue? Making the more difficult choice was one of the wisest of my life. It was *beshert* (providential), and it came in the form of a red rose."

The guideposts directing us on our life's journey take many forms.

HEART TO HEART

Bill Eaton

Things were not going well for Bill Eaton in late 1991. He had undergone bypass surgery in 1988, but his heart was still in bad shape. He was in the intensive care unit when Mrs. Leslie Tillman, the transplant coordinator came to his bed. It was 8:00 P.M.

"Are you ready?" she asked.

"For what?"

"We have a heart for you and are taking you to get it. It is from a seventeen-year-old young man by the name of Allen who was in a terrible automobile accident."

"I had mixed emotions and was very apprehensive, realizing that my heart was about to be cut from my body. I prayed, saying, 'this is too much for me to handle. I need help.' Almost immediately I felt a calmness envelop me."

After Bill's successful surgery, he wrote a letter of thanks to the donor's family. He wished to thank them personally, but in order to conform to the rules of confidentiality, the request had to be sent through the local transplant office and the office to which the donor's family was connected. Since his letter had been misfiled it took three years before Bill received a positive response. "We would very much like to meet you," they replied, "Please call us to make the arrangements." They lived in Ti, Oklahoma, three hundred fifty miles from Memphis.

Allen's mother, Linda, shared the following information with Bill:

"When Allen was four or five, we took him to California where he saw the ocean for the first time and where he developed a love of water. As a young teenager, he enjoyed going to Arlington, Texas, to visit Six Flags Over Texas. Six months before he died, he came to Memphis where he visited Graceland, Beale Street, and where he played basketball in the Pyramid with his high school team.

These were the places he loved best.

When he died, we were told that his liver went to a recipient in Texas; his kidneys to California; and his heart to you, in Memphis."

In telling this story and granting permission for its inclusion here, Bill added the following: "On my third visit to Ti, I met some of Allen's friends and other recipients of his organs. I was introduced to a pretty young woman named Gail who held her small son on her hip as she stood before me with her husband.

'I was Allen's girlfriend since we were in the fourth grade. I loved him and still miss him very much. I have a favor to ask,' she said. 'Would you mind if I put my ear to your chest so I could listen to his heart?'

I am indebted to Charles Steinberg who introduced me to Mr. Eaton. Charles is the oldest recipient of a liver transplant in Memphis. He continues to devote many hours weekly to reassuring prospective liver donors and their recipients.

GUESTS

Rabbi Rafael Grossman

Walking along Amsterdam Avenue on the upper west side of New York, my wife and I met an old friend, Rabbi Rafael G. Grossman. "Rabbi," I declared, "someone mentioned that you had a compelling story. Would you share it with us?"

"Of course," he replied. "It happened many years ago when we brought our family to New York. We opted to have dinner prior to driving to our apartment. Arriving there, I opened the trunk of the rental car to find all of our possessions missing. It was upsetting to lose our clothing, but my greatest concern was for the irreplaceable personal items that had belonged to my father, of blessed memory."

"Twelve years later, I conducted a seminar in Memphis with visitors who headed Judaic studies programs throughout the country. Prior to the Sabbath, I received a telephone call from a participant advising that she was Sabbath observant. She requested a place to stay where she could have kosher food, and she accepted the invitation to stay at our home. A couple of hours later, she called again to tell me she had met another participant who was observant. I asked her to invite him to stay with us too."

"The following day both joined us at Sabbath services held at our synagogue. Afterwards, our gentleman guest excitedly approached me with the following account:

'I heard your Hebrew name called prior to your reciting the blessing,' the man said, 'and I have something to tell you. Years ago, while shopping in a Judaic shop in New York, a man came in. He held up a large brown paper bag and yelled out, "How much will you give me for this stuff?"'

"The owner replied, 'I won't pay anything for items that were obviously stolen.'"

"The man wadded up the bag and threw it at my feet before running away. When I began examining its contents, I found a set of *t'fillin* (phylacteries), a *tallis* (prayer shawl), and an ancient and valuable book. Since the only identification was a Hebrew name in the *tallis* bag, I was unable to return these things to their rightful owner until I heard your name called this morning."

Rabbi Grossman was the chief rabbi of the Baron Hirsch Synagogue in Memphis, Tennessee, when it was the largest orthodox synagogue in America. He served as president of the Rabbinic Council of America and the head of the Beth Din of America. He has recently been asked to serve as chancellor of a new university in Israel. After the loss of our son, he and I established Chai, Inc., a multi-faceted social support system to help families with catastrophically stricken children.

In 1986 he came to New York to lend spiritual support to my son, my wife, and me while we were in the city for our son's treatment at the Sloan-Kettering Cancer Institute.

TAXI DRIVERS

Harry Samuels

While Jeffery Feld and I were attending a meeting in Philadelphia, he received an urgent telephone call from his wife, Susan. She had gone to the Jacob Javits Center in New York City to attend a meeting and had left her billfold with all of her money in the back seat of a taxicab. Before she could cancel her credit cards, she was paged. When she came to the front desk, she saw the taxi driver. He handed her the missing billfold and refused to accept a reward.

An Israeli lady found that her desperately ill daughter required a surgical procedure that could be done only in New York City. Additionally, it was to cost $250,000. She was of modest means and had exhausted all charitable sources. As a last resort she began going from door to door—pleading for help.

One evening after collecting a substantial sum, she accidentally left the paper bag of money in the taxi. She was in a panic when the doorbell rang. It was the taxi driver who returned her money. He refused to accept a reward. He explained that he only drove at night, and that she was his last passenger that day. When he arrived home he discovered the paper bag filled with money, and he immediately drove to her apartment to return it.

Tearfully, the lady told him, "I can only bless you and your family with all my heart."

The following day the cab driver didn't feel well. He called his boss and told him he would not be able to come to his office. It was located at the World Trade Center, and the date was September 11, 2001.

New York cab drivers bear the brunt of countless jokes and bad publicity. There are, no doubt, many stories similar to these that are never told.

Following college graduation and prior to my induction into the army, I drove a Yellow Taxicab in St. Louis, Missouri, for three weeks. One of my first fares was a gentleman who entered my cab saying, "Take me to a matinee." As I was young and inexperienced, I proceeded to drive to Grand Avenue where I stopped at the Fox Theater." What is this?" he asked. I replied, 'It's the only show playing around here.' "What are you, a wise guy?" he yelled, jumping out and slamming the door! Clearly, I had taken his request literally rather than as a euphemism for an afternoon romance.

When St. Louis cab drivers weren't busy, they would often park and congregate near street corners, sharing their interesting experiences. When they ran out of their own stories, they would repeat others they had heard. One day I heard someone telling my own story.

BRIDAL PARTY

Jon Greenberg

Jon Greenberg, who provided this story, was the ring-bearer at the wedding of Kate and Ben Sheon in 1929. He was four years old and he escorted a four-year-old flower girl.

Seven years ago the former flower girl met Kate in Florida. "How would you like to meet the boy with whom you walked down the aisle sixty-five years ago," Kate asked.

"No thanks," she responded. "We already have enough friends down here."

"You're making a big mistake," retorted Kate. "Jon and Adelyn are an outstanding couple and I know you would love them."

"You must be kidding," she replied. "We're having dinner with them tomorrow. We've been good friends since 1947, but neither Jon nor I recalled our first connection."

THE BRIDGE HAND

Richard Oshlag

This story began in 1978 with a telephone call to Richard Oshlag from his friend Alfred Sheinwold in Los Angles.

"A man named Moritz Oschlag, whose last name is almost the same as yours, just painted my house. Are you by chance related?" he asked.

"I don't believe so," Richard replied, "but I'll ask my sister Joan who's a history buff to check on it."

Joan learned that the housepainter had come to America from Denmark in 1945 and that his ten siblings lived in Copenhagen. His father came to Denmark from Poland in 1905. Joan began writing to the family in Denmark to learn if she and they were related, but she was never able to establish a family relationship with them.

While playing in the North American Open Pairs Bridge Final in 1986, Richard played a hand so well it was recorded in international bridge publications. Carl Oschlag read the story in a Swedish bridge bulletin. He sent a letter to the American Contract Bridge League asking it to be forwarded to Richard Oshlag, unaware that Richard worked for the A.C.B.L. "Are you related to Moritz Oschlag or do you know of him?" the letter asked.

Carl had not seen or heard from Moritz since before World War II.

Thanks to the telephone call ten years earlier from Mr. Sheinwold, Richard did know of Moritz, but neither he nor his sister could locate him. He had vanished.

A month later Joan received a telephone call from Leeza Oschlag who was investigating her own family history. She was the daughter of Moritz and had been told that Joan's computer held all of the Oschlag family's genealogy.

"Where is your father?" asked Joan.

"He's retired and living in Portland, Oregon," she answered.

Joan immediately contacted Carl with the information he had been seeking.

Thanks to a bridge hand, Carl Oschlag was reunited with his brother Moritz after a forty-year separation.

The following is the deal that reunited a family:

```
Dir: East          ♠ A Q 10 4
                   ♥ K 7 3
                   ♦ A 10 4
                   ♣ Q 9 4
♠ 9 5                           ♠ 7 6 3 2
♥ 8 6 4                         ♥ A J 10 5 2
♦ Q J 7 3 2                     ♦ 9 5
♣ K 7 3                         ♣ 10 6
                   ♠ K J 8
                   ♥ Q 9
                   ♦ K 8 6
                   ♣ A J 8 5 2
```

WEST	NORTH	EAST	SOUTH
		Pass	1 ♣
1 ♦	Dbl	1 ♥	1 NT
Pass	3 NT	All Pass	

Richard is the first to agree that an opening 1 NT bid would have fared better—East-West probably wouldn't have been in the bidding. But Oshlag's immediate task was to make his notrump game after West led the heart 8.

East put the heart 10 on the opening lead—but Oshlag ducked. East correctly returned his fourth-best heart, and this time Oshlag had to win. He overtook the queen with dummy's king and led another heart! When East cashed out with his hearts, Oshlag discarded a diamond and a club from dummy and three small clubs from the closed hand.

When a club was led at trick six, Richard won the club A and claimed the contract on a Vienna Coup, correctly assessing that West had the only protection in both minors. He said to his LHO, "If you don't have five diamonds and the club king for your overcall, I give up!"

Richard Oshlag is considered to be one of the top bridge players in Memphis and among the best in the country.

THE BOOK COVER

Harry Samuels

"We need a cover for the new book," I recently advised my wife Flora. "I have an idea for a picture, but it involves driving to Arkansas. Are you game?"

It was Thanksgiving and a warm, fall day. We loaded a ladder into the rear of our van and headed across the Mississippi River. As we approached a visitor's center near West Memphis, Flora suggested we stop for some local input.

As I approached a man who was polishing a display case he asked, "Can I be of help?" "We have a strange request," I replied. "Can you direct us to the intersection of two highways located nearby that do not have much traffic?" He pointed on a map to a location four miles away. "That should do the trick."

We thanked him, but before leaving the building he asked where we lived. He said he was required to enter the name of each visitor's community in a daily log. I told him we lived in Memphis, but that I had lived in Jonesboro, Arkansas many years ago.

"I'm from Jonesboro," he said.

When I asked his name he replied, "Harper."

"I was in the Jaycees with Bob Harper approximately forty-eight years ago." I told him. "He and I helped build the town's Little League baseball field."

With a big smile he responded, "Bob's my dad,"

After a short drive, we came to the recommended site. Flora climbed the ladder we set next to the highway and took a picture of me standing in the middle of the intersection. The image we wished to convey was that of someone standing at the crossroads of his life. That is the picture we used for this cover.

PART VIII
ISRAEL

TO SAVE A LIFE

Baruch Gordon

Dov, a young soldier serving in the Israeli army, was manning an isolated guard post in Hebron when an Arab sniper shot him. With no one to help him and unable to call for help, it was likely that he would bleed to death before he could be found. Another soldier fortunately heard the shot and rushed to investigate. He spotted Dov on the ground bleeding profusely. He immediately administered first aid to stop the flow of blood and called for an ambulance. When medical help arrived, he left without leaving his name.

Eventually Dov was treated at a medical facility. The doctors told Dov's parents that had it not been for the immediate and appropriate actions of the other soldier, their son would not have survived. The grateful parents felt it was indeed a miracle that their son's benefactor had heard what no one else had heard that night. They tried to locate him to express their gratitude, but he had left the area. During Dov's recovery, his family contacted army officials to learn the name of the soldier who had saved their son's life, but no one knew him. The parents posted a sign in the tiny grocery store they operated in Kiryat Malachi. They described the miracle that had occurred and asked for information about the man—hoping for a lead to find him.

A year later, a woman entered their store and noticed the sign. "I believe my son Doron is the one you're seeking," she said. "I recall him telling me of a similar incident in which he was involved." She called her son on her cell phone. "Yes," she told them, "He remembers the incident quite well. He was the one who had saved Dov's life."

Soon all the local families gathered for a joyful celebration and to express thanks to the stranger on behalf of her son. One of those present knew of an additional reason to celebrate.

Doron's mother pulled Dov's mother aside to say, "I came here today for a specific purpose. You don't remember me, but twenty years ago, I stood in your store feeling great stress. You and your husband noticed how sad I looked and asked me what was the matter. I explained that I was pregnant and overwhelmed.

There were so many unbearable difficulties—financial, social, and emotional. I had decided to have an abortion. You both stopped everything and listened calmly and lovingly to my problems. You offered much encouragement and support. Because of you, everything began to look different, and I chose to keep my baby. I no longer live around here, but I happened to be passing through. I thought it would be nice to visit your store and thank you for all your help. The name of that precious baby who would not have been born had it not been for you is my nineteen year-old son, Doron.

The above names have been changed, but several individuals have attested to the facts. Our friend, Baruch Gordon, the English editor of Arutz Sheva (channel seven) of Israel National News, granted permission to use this remarkable story.

THE COFFEE SET

Aviva Garfine

While on a trip to Florida in 2005, my wife and I visited an impressive commercial development in West Palm Beach called City Place. One of its most attractive stores, Ahava, is an outstanding Judaica shop.

While browsing in their extensive book department, I told the saleslady, Aviva Garfine, that I had written a book called *Beshert*. I asked if they would be interested in stocking it. After I had explained the basics of the book, she said, "Tell me one of your stories." When I had finished, she introduced me to their book buyer who agreed to stock my book. Later, Aviva shared the following personal experience:

"Two years ago while on a trip to Israel, I fell in love with a most unusual Turkish coffee set. It was displayed in the front window of a Jerusalem shop, but it was the Sabbath and the store was closed. I returned the following day, but the store was still closed. As we were leaving the next day, I abandoned the idea of obtaining it.

Recently, an employee of a local agency that helps arrange missions to Israel called, "There's a young man in Palm Beach who's never been to the Holy Land. He'd like to travel with us, but he can't afford the cost. Would you be willing to help him?"

"I told her that I would pay for his trip with one stipulation,—that he not be given the name of his sponsor.

A month later the mission director again called me." "The gentleman returned from the trip," she began; "he was extremely impressed with both the trip and your generosity," she continued. "I would appreciate your stopping by my office to pick up a note of thanks and gift he brought for his benefactress."

"My curiosity turned to amazement as I unwrapped the container and found the Turkish coffee set."

THE TALMUD

Rabbi Efraim Greenblatt

Efraim Greenblatt was sixteen years old in 1948, but he was already a seasoned veteran in Israel's fight to become a nation. He was a messenger for Yitzhak Shamir, who headed an underground faction bent on gaining control of Palestine from the British. (Shamir later became the Prime Minister of Israel.)

"We were in an area called Lifta. It was located near the highway leading to Tel Aviv—now the western part of Jerusalem. Our quarters were in a small wooden building. Aware of the Biblical injunction to study Torah whenever possible, I brought two volumes of the Talmud, the Oral Law, for study during free time. I placed them on a board above some bricks next to my cot.

That evening we were attacked late at night. There were lots of bullets flying, but we managed to drive back the enemy. The next morning I decided to study my books. It was then I discovered the bullets meant for me. They had become embedded in one of the tractates of the Talmud. It had saved my life."

Rabbi Greenblatt is a world-renowned Torah scholar. He has written seventeen scholarly books that have been reprinted many times. He is a gentle-natured person who has devoted his life to study and acts of loving-kindness for all the people of Memphis and beyond.

During the Israeli War of Independence, he served as a member of "Lechi," the most radical segment of fighters. Lechi was convinced that the British had to be expelled before the state could be established. Skirmishes between Lechi and Haganah, the British-recognized Jewish defense force, continued until Lechi submitted to Hagannah's unified command.

Many years later, while in Memphis, Rabbi Greenblatt came to our home to meet Professor Yigal Yadin. My wife and I had established a chapter of the American Friends for Hebrew University, and Professor Yadin, who headed the Department of Archeology at Hebrew University, was our guest speaker. As a member of Hagannah, he had served as chief of staff of the Israeli army and later as deputy prime minister. The picture I took of them sitting next to each other while smiling, belies the fact that they had once served in fighting groups at odds with each other.

"IZZY"

Harry Samuels

For the past fifteen years Yitzach "Izzy" Assour has come to Memphis, Tennessee. He has displayed works of art created by Israeli soldiers, art they had been encouraged to produce as occupational therapy, while recovering from their wounds.

We have remained good friends since his first visit. Recently we noticed one of his sculptures depicting a circle of figures whose arms blended into each other. It was a very moving bronze sculpture expressing a universal concept of people connecting.

Izzy had just finished dinner at our home when I commented on his creation. "I didn't know you were so talented," I said, "Your sculpture is magnificent. It reminds me of a similar one I once saw."

I told him of our visit to Israel in 1981. We had come for the bar mitzvah of our youngest son, David, of blessed memory. The president of Israel, Yitzak Navon, had invited us to visit his home. As we entered, we noticed a small sculpture resting on a table to the left of the front door. It made such an impression on us, we photographed it and have told others of it. "It was a smaller version of your sculpture we saw today. Did you obtain permission to use it as a model?" I asked.

"It wasn't necessary," he replied. "I was the artist. I gave it to Israel and titled it, All of Us."

THE STRANGER

Louis Kotler

While studying with Rabbi Efraim Greenblatt, he was interrupted by a telephone call from Mr. Louis Kotler. Rabbi Greenblatt repeated their conversation. I was intrigued and called Mr. Kotler the following day for some clarification and permission to use it in a manuscript. Mr. Kotler, who is now deceased, agreed to allow the publication of this anecdote. Here is the story in his words:

We had traveled to Israel to attend the formal dedication of a new wing of the Shaare Zedek Hospital. A friend had arranged for me to meet with a well-known member of the Knesset [the legislative body of Israel], but our meeting was cancelled at the last moment. I was disappointed because we were returning to Memphis in two days.

Saturday morning, I walked to the Great Synagogue in Jerusalem for prayer services. As I entered the sanctuary, I asked an official at the door if I could be given the honor of reciting a blessing prior to the reading of the Torah, [the sacred scroll containing the *Five Books of Moses,* a portion of which is recited each Saturday and Monday morning.] I was ushered to a seat at the front of the synagogue.

A gentleman sitting next to me said, "You must be from America?"

"How did you know," I asked.

"You're wearing a suit and tie. As you can see, we dress more casually here."

"I'm from Memphis, Tennessee," I replied.

"Oh,' he offered, "That's across the river from Arkansas isn't it?"

"Have you ever been to Memphis?" I queried.

"No," he replied, "I've been to Washington D.C., Los Angeles, New York, Chicago, Detroit and Cleveland, but never to Memphis."

"I assumed he was probably in the import-export business."

"What brings you to Israel?" he asked.

"I came for the dedication of the new hospital wing. Tell me, do you contribute to the Shaare Zedek Hospital?"

"Yes," he replied.

"I buy Israel bonds. Do you buy them too?" I questioned.

"Yes, I support the sale of bonds."

"But when my bonds mature, I donate them to Hadassah Hospital. Do you support Hadassah Hospital?"

"Certainly," the man replied, "I help the Hadassah Hospital whenever I can."

"So tell me, what do you do for a living?"

The stranger looked down sheepishly and softly replied, "I am Ephraim Katzir, the president of Israel."

Mr. Kotler thought the man was kidding until he too was called forth to deliver a blessing. As he stood, a plaque was revealed on his chair stating that it was the traditional seat of the President.

THE POWER OF PRAYER

Dr. Yehudah Farkash

Dr. Yehudah Farkash is a physician living in Bar Kahn, a small village in southern Israel. His wife, Dalai, is a surgical nurse. It was a cold, rainy November day and they had been ministering to their desperately ill neighbor, Dov, who refused to be taken to the hospital.

Reluctantly leaving their sick friend, the Farkash couple drove to Jerusalem to pick up their sister-in-law and her newborn and take them to Tel Aviv. Upon their arrival in Tel Aviv, they were informed that their friend, Dov, had died.

Piling back into their car, they immediately drove home to be of help to Dov's family. As they entered Dov's house, Yehudah went to the room containing Dov's remains. He recited *Tehillim(Psalms)* until 11:30 p.m., awaiting the arrival of the burial society. (The body is not to be left alone until burial, and *Psalms* are continuously recited. *Psalms* are also read on behalf of very ill individuals and at critical times in a person's life. Many believe the recitation of these prayers can have profound positive effects).

While enroute to Jerusalem Yehudah and Dalai had listened to the news broadcasts on their car radio. They'd heard of the torrential rains in the south and of the dangerous driving conditions. "Four soldiers," they heard, "were being rescued by a helicopter from a swollen stream." Although Yehudah was unaware of it, the ranking officer of the four was Ronnie, his youngest brother.

Ronnie managed to arrange the rescue of his three men by helicopter, but the pilot was unable to help him since another person was needed to help lower and raise the cables from the aircraft.

Joseph was a veteran at air rescue operations, but because of the Sabbath, he was at his home when he heard the broadcast seeking assistance. He immediately jumped into his car and drove to a landing site that had not yet been inundated. He was in such a hurry, he came without a uniform, barefoot, and without proper identification. The first pilot he approached refused to take him aboard, but he convinced another pilot to allow him to help. With great effort, and against great odds, they recovered Ronnie.

It was not until 6 a.m. the following day that Ronnie called Yehudah to tell of his narrow escape. "It was miraculous," Ron told his brother. "Joseph saved my life."

"You are wrong," Yedudah, answered. "Dov saved your life through the Tehillim that was recited for him."

AT THE DENTIST'S

Harry Samuels

As my dentist, Dr. Plesofsky, worked on my teeth, he mentioned that he and his wife were planning a trip to Israel. "I told another patient, Jimmy Jalenak, of our plans," he said, "and Jimmy then shared an experience with me that he had while on a similar trip in 1976. He told me of the antics of someone from Memphis—I don't know his name—and of a funny incident that happened on that trip."

"There were forty people on our bus," Jimmy began, "and one man in our group soon began speaking a few words of Yiddish with the driver. We assumed they were speaking Hebrew, and for several days—whenever our guide was not present—we would ask our companion to translate such things as signs on store windows. Although he could read (but not understand) Hebrew, he decided to play a joke on us by giving us quick and authoritative-sounding answers to our queries.

Late one night after our wives had gone to bed, he and I went for a walk behind our hotel that was located on the summit of Mt. Carmel overlooking the beautiful city of Haifa. I smoked cigarettes at that time and used wooden kitchen matches to light them.

As we strolled, I noticed an iron post with writing on it sticking out of the ground. It had some Hebrew letters, and I was sure it was a monument of some sort since during that week our guide had pointed out so many monuments wherever we traveled. I held a lit match near it and asked him to translate the inscription. He bent down to examine it while I continued to provide matches so we could see what was written. He seemed to struggle with the wording, as we edged closer trying to determine its significance. (Actually he was trying to think of something plausible to tell me since he couldn't very well say it was an ice-cream parlor or bowling alley.) As I began to run out of matches a lady walking by asked if she could be of help. I told her my friend was trying to read the words on what I assumed to be a small monument."

"Let's see," she offered, as I lit a final match for her. "It says GAS LINE!"

"During breakfast the following day I told others in our group what had happened. When everyone realized our friend couldn't translate Hebrew and had been fooling us all week he lost his credibility, and when he boarded the bus that morning, he was greeted with silence."

As he removed the implements from my mouth, Dr. Plesofsky said, "I'm going to ask Jimmy the name of that guy. He must be some character."

"You're going to find this hard to believe," I said, "but I was that character!"

AFTERWORD

Not everyone embraces the concept of synchronicity—that there is purpose in our life experiences. A plethora of distinguished authors and thinkers attribute connections such as those described in my text to a variety of causes other than synchronicity.

Malcolm Gladwell in his book, *The Tipping Point: How Little Things Can Make a Big Difference,* suggests that what many see as meaningful coincidences (synchronicity) are merely the result of randomness. "When viewing two events," he says, "our bias is to immediately establish a causal link."

In his book *Innumeracy*, John Allen Paulos claims, "Our minds are intent on discovering meaning where there is only probability."

Nossim N. Taleb in *Fooled by Randomness: The Hidden Role of Chance in Life and In the Markets* points out that the chance of winning the New Jersey lottery is one in 170,000,000. Yet it happened twice to Evelyn Adams. Another lady recently won the New York lottery for the second time in four years.

Andrew Newberg, M.D, in his book, *Why God Won't Go Away,* describes recent studies by Peter Brugger, Ph.D., of University Hospital, Zurich, Switzerland, who determined that some people are more inclined to see meaning and significance in chance events because of their elevated levels of dopamine, a neurochemical that helps us recognize patterns.

Ruma Falk of Hebrew University, a world-renowned specialist in probabilistic thinking, studied numerous stories of coincidence. In *The Surprisingness of Coincidences*, he suggests that people are amazed when faced with a coincidence because they underestimate the total number of surprising possibilities, or the number of pairs that can be formed from a specific number of objects. "Having a friend who knows someone, who knows someone you know, is not as rare as one might suppose, because that set of people could comprise a group [that includes] roughly half the population of the United States." He further notes in a 1983 article in the *Journal of the American Statistical Association* that "the model for studying coincidences includes the Law of Truly Large Numbers. It posits: When enormous numbers of events, people, and their interactions, accumulate over time, almost any outrageous event is bound to occur.

Most of us accept the idea that all things are possible but many are unlikely to happen. That an infinite number of chimpanzees, with typewriters or word processors, over an infinite period of time, would write *Hamlet* is theoretically possible. But it is so ludicrous that it cannot be considered seriously.

On the other hand, many believe that randomness and probability do not negate the concept of an ordered universe but are a part of it. According to Zaddok Hakohen of Lublin, the nineteenth-century sage, "The first premise of faith is to believe that there is no such thing as happenstance ... every detail, small or great, they are all from the Holy One."

The idea of purpose and order in life experiences continues to assert itself. Although theories of randomness and probability can be applied to most of the anecdotes in my books, some of the stories included seem so far-fetched that one might as readily explain them in accordance with Arthur Koestler's belief expressed in his book, *The Roots of Coincidence*. "There may be a universal hanging-together of things imbedded in a universal matrix."

Peter Jordan, in his book, *The Mystery of Chance*, views such events as being bound together by cosmic glue into a meaningful and coherent pattern.

Dr. Karl Pibram, professor of neuropsychology at Stanford University, suggests "the brain may be a type of hologram, a pattern and frequency analyzer, which creates hard reality by interpreting frequencies from a dimension beyond space and time."

The astrophysicist, Dr. Michael Shallis, in his book, *On Time: An Investigation Into Scientific Knowledge and Human Experience*, states: "Some argue that statistics of probability are appropriate in a controlled laboratory situation or when dealing with large numbers of similar events, but are inappropriate for unrepeatable, subjective, real-life experiences. In dealing with unique events, in hindsight, there is no sensible or meaningful way of estimating their likelihood."

Taking into account the work of the foregoing scientists, Jordan concludes that, "We may soon uncover evidence that the universe functions so as to unify matter, energy and consciousness, and that synchronous events will be liberated from the stigma of occultism and will no longer be seen as disturbing."

Sir Winston Churchill in the book *Great Destiny* asserts: "The longer one lives, the more one realizes that everything depends upon chance, and the harder it is to believe that this omnipotent factor in human affairs arises simply from the blind interplay of events. Chance, Fortune, Luck, Destiny, Fate, Providence seem to me only different ways of expressing the same thing, to wit, that a man's own contribution to his life story is continually dominated by an external superior power."

Why do we choose a certain route, and not another, that unexpectedly leads us to an answer? Why do we miss or cancel a particular appointment that leads to harm, or benefit? What causes us to speak to or help a stranger who turns out to be important to our lives? What leads us to the circumstances through which we find our soul mate, our friends, our life's work? In such instances and many others, are our lives governed by the aforementioned fate, destiny, or divine providence suggested by Sir Winston Churchill as well as some of the scientists cited above, or by the laws of probability and blind chance? Is there purpose in our existence and a reason for everything that happens, or are we subject only to the randomness of luck?

My books are not meant to answer these questions but rather to raise them. I intend them to entertain and to elicit thought-provoking insights. May *Crossroads* succeed in this regard, and may it help to make you more aware of the pleasures of reaching out to others and of discovering the synchronicities in your own life.

Some readers point out that, unlike life experiences, the stories included in my books end happily. It is true that life can be grim. The person who cancelled his reservation on a flight that crashed might have provided a seat for someone who otherwise would have been saved. As I wrote in *Beshert,* "Life is a divine symphony with lots of harmony we call happiness and lots of dissonance we call pain and suffering, all under the direction of the Composer who is the only one who knows the entire score."

Harry Samuels

WORKS CITED

Churchill, Sir Winston. *Great Destiny*. New York: G.P. Putnam's Sons, 1965.

Cohen, Brad. *Front of the Class*: How Tourette Syndrome Made Me the Teacher I Never Had. Acton, MA: VanderWyk and Burnham, 2005.

Falk, Ruma, & MacGregor, D. *The Surprisingness of Coincidences*. New York: North Holland, 1983.

—. *Journal of American Statistical Association*: Volume 84, No. 408, December 1989.

Frager, Stanley R. *The Champion Within You: How to Overcome Problems, Obstacles and Adversity in Your Life*. Louisville: Champion, 1992.

Friedman, Thomas L. *The World is Flat: A Brief History of the Twenty-First Century*. New York: Farrar, Strauss and Giroux, 2005.

Gilder, George. *Naked Nomads: Unmarried Men in America*. New York: New York Times Book Co, 1974.

Ginsberg, Scott. *Hello My Name is Scott*. Portland, OR.: Front Porch Publishing, 2002.

Gladwell, Malcolm. *The Tipping Point: How Little Things Can Make a Big Difference*. New York: Little, Brown and Company, 2000.

Koestler, Arthur. *The Roots of Coincidence*. New York: Vintage.1973.

Kushner, Lawrence. *Invisible Lines of Connection*. Woodstock, VT.: Lights Publishing, 1996.

Mirvis, Tova. *The Outside World*. New York: A. Knopf, 2004.

Putnam, Robert D. *Bowling Alone: The Collapse and Revival of American Community*. New York: Simon and Schuster, 2000.

—. *Better Together: Restoring the American Community.* New York: Simon and Schuster, 2003.

Rosenthal, Bob. *From Passaic to the Moon: An Insider's True Adventures.* Funkstown, MD. Star-L Publishing, 2001.

Roth, Zev. *Monsey, Kiryat Sefer, and Beyond.* Southfield, MI.: Targum/Feldheim, 2005.

Samuels, Harry. *Beshert: True Stories of Connections.* New York: I Universe, 2004.

Shallis, Dr. Michael D. *On Time: An Investigation Into Scientific Knowledge and Human Experience.* New York: Shocken, 1983.

Taleb, Nassim N. *Fooled by Randomness: The Hidden Role of Chance in Life and in the Markets.* New York: Texere, 2004.

Vaughan, Alan. *Incredible Coincidence: The Baffling World of Synchronicity.* New York: Ballantine Books, 1979.

Weisberg, Chana. *Divine Whispers-Stories That Speak to the Heart and Soul.* Southfield, MI.: Targum/Feldheim, 2005.

Wiesel, Elie. *Night.* New York: Bantam Books, 1982.

978-0-595-42579-2
0-595-42579-8

Printed in the United States
75034LV00002B/511-570